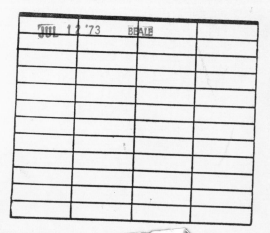

JUL 1 2 '73	BEALE		

DAYS OF THRILLS AND ADVENTURE

ALAN G. BARBOUR

DAYS OF THRILLS AND ADVENTURE

THE MACMILLAN COMPANY

COLLIER-MACMILLAN LIMITED, LONDON

The Macmillan Company
866 Third Avenue, New York, N.Y. 10022
Collier-Macmillan Canada Ltd., Toronto, Ontario

Library of Congress Catalog Card Number: 79-120345

FIRST PRINTING

Printed in the United States of America

Dedicated to the memory of
ROY BARCROFT, 1902-1969
*   in grateful appreciation for*
presenting all of us with so many wonderful
Days of Thrills and Adventure

ACKNOWLEDGMENTS

The author wishes to express his sincere thanks to the individuals and organizations listed below who supplied, through the years, the stills and information which have made this book possible.

The Individuals:
Roy Barcroft, Spencer Gordon Bennet, John Cocchi, Edward Connor, Homer Dickens, William K. Everson, Phil Glickman, Eric Hoffman, Henry Kier, Al Kilgore, Ernie Kirkpatrick, Paula Klaw, William Lava, Milton Luboviski, Louis McMahon, Bob Miller, Gray Morrow, Sloan Nibley, Bob Price, Mark Ricci, Gene Ringgold, Stephen Sally, Samuel M. Sherman, Jim Shoenberger, Tom Steele, Chris Steinbrunner, Linda Stirling, and Bud Thackery.

The Organizations:
Cinemabilia, Collector's Bookstore, Columbia Pictures Corporation, Fawcett Publications, Inc., Kier's, King Features Syndicate, Larry Edmunds Bookshop, Marvel Comics Group, The Memory Shop, Movie Star News, The Museum of Modern Art, National Periodical Publications, Inc., National Telefilm Associates, Screen Gems, Inc., United Features Syndicate, Inc., Universal Pictures Corporation, and Vista Productions.

With Special Thanks to:
Jean Barbour and James Robert Parish.

Contents

Preface   BUSTER CRABBE   *xi*

Author's Note   *xiii*

Introduction   WILLIAM K. EVERSON   *xv*

 1   The First Episode   *1*

 2   The Early-Talkie and Independent Serials   *11*

 3   Republic Enters the Scene   *19*

 4   Comic Strips on the Screen   *27*

 5   The Descendants of Zorro   *39*

 6   Science Fiction   *47*

 7   Hit the Saddle   *59*

 8   From Radio and the Pulps   *71*

 9   A Stock Company of Villains   *81*

10   The Serial Heroes   *91*

11   . . . and the Heroines   *101*

12   Jungle Jeopardy   *111*

13   The Stunt Men   *119*

14   World War II   *133*

15   They Got Their Men   *139*

16   Behind the Mask   *147*

17   The Final Episode   *155*

18   The Great Serial Revival of 1965–66   *159*

Appendix   *163*

Preface

ALAN BARBOUR's BOOK is thoroughly enjoyable, and I am happy
and proud to have been a part of those *Days of Thrills and
Adventure* he describes so well.

In page after page I was treated to a pleasantly nostalgic
backward look at friends and acquaintances, actors and actresses
with whom I share the common bond of those hectic but
happy days of movie-making.

I cannot recommend the book highly enough. It is accurate,
interesting, and entertaining. It should find an enthusiastic audience
of remember-those-good-old-days moviegoers, as well as
serious film buffs and students.

BUSTER CRABBE

Author's Note

"IT SEEMS LIKE ONLY YESTERDAY!" I wonder how many people have uttered that now-trite phrase as they fondly recalled the wonderful memories of years gone by. I had always assumed that it was a phrase reserved for those "senior citizens" who had little else to do with their time but spend it recalling the glorious days they would never see again. But now I find that at the ripe old age of thirty-seven I am already uttering that same woeful cry myself.

It does, indeed, seem like only yesterday that a freckle-faced, red-haired boy by the name of Alan G. Barbour practically ran those few short blocks from his home on Linden Street to the Broadway Theatre in downtown Oakland, California, every Saturday, timing his arrival so that he could get his two bags of fresh popcorn and still be seated in time to see the serial at twelve-twenty and again about three-thirty.

Yes, they were wonderful days. And, of course, the serials didn't end with those two screenings. I lived every episode for a full seven days until the next one flashed on the screen. I made my Captain Marvel cape and my Spy Smasher cape and I fought a thousand mock battles with boyhood companions.

Those days, perhaps the most enjoyable of my life, are gone now—and the serials are gone, just as the pulp magazines and the radio adventure shows vanished before them. The serials brought me, and millions like me, pleasure beyond verbal description— and now they're gone, forever, and I feel sorry, not for myself, for I enjoyed them all, but for all those future generations of young boys who will never experience the joy of sharing those wonderful Saturday afternoons with bigger-than-life heroes on the screen and reliving all those unforgettable *Days of Thrills and Adventure.*

ALAN G. BARBOUR, 1970

Introduction

Days of Thrills and Adventure seems a particularly felicitous title for Mr. Barbour's excursion into the color and history of the American chapter-play. Were the book called, for example, "The Art of the Serial," the author would be in the defensive position of having to prove that there *is* an art to the serial! But I think the key word is "Days"; when all is said and done, no American serial really lives up to its reputation, or to our own nostalgic recollections of it. The good serials—and there are some *very* good ones—more often than not survive on merits that we didn't even dream existed when we first saw them. To be enjoyed to the full, the serial had to be seen in those days paralleling our own days of innocence, when the movies truly had magic, when we believed everything that we saw on the screen, and when, in our happy ignorance of critical standards or technical knowledge, the serial was judged by the same standards as a box-office blockbuster or an artistic masterpiece—and usually survived the comparison rather well.

It is sometimes surprising what aspects of the serial (or any film, for that matter) can impress themselves indelibly on the mind of a child. My own most vivid recollections of serials from the early thirties are not of the chases and fights and marathons of action, but rather of climaxes that approached moments of near-horror. One jungle serial reached its climax with the hero being buried alive by natives in a deep pit; the framing of the shot and the rising crescendo of beating drums are details as vivid in my memory now as

they were nearly forty years ago, and I can still sense the feeling of claustrophobic horror that the scene created. (I have never seen that chapter again, nor have I ever tried to trace the serial, although since the period is so clearly defined, it would have to be one of a mere half-dozen titles. But some memories are too delicious to disturb, and why take the risk?) In that same period, Universal's science-fiction serial *Vanishing Shadow* (1934) was productive of a similar traumatic experience. One of the "good" scientists had perfected some kind of electrical death-ray which was installed at the door to his laboratory. After it was tried out amid a shower of sparks, the scientist told his cohort that the ray would certainly kill any crook who came through that door. Needless to say, within the reel either the heroine or the hero blundered through that door, to be enveloped in electrical sparks for the fadeout. I never had a chance to see the follow-up chapter, but I was comforted by the preparatory remark that the death-ray was designed to kill "crooks"; that was the obvious escape clause, and I imparted to that death-ray the ability to distinguish between good and evil, the right to exercise judgment on who should live and who should die. I am sure that the ultimate solution was a much more mechanical one—yet again, my own innocence and awe made those few seconds of film immortal. Later on, when violence and horror were less common in the serial—and less likely anyway to create such deeply etched impressions on the mind of a maturing ten-year-old—the memories formed were rather different.

Curiously, I remember *The Lone Ranger,* one of the best Western serials, not for its action or even for its quite strong story-line. The impression that lingers is a rather stylistic one revolving around the dominance of the color white: the white stetsons, white silk shirts, and white horses of the rangers, the white chalk cliffs and white sands of the locations. The serial has been unavailable for reappraisal for some time, but logic insists that Republic undoubtedly used their standard locations in and around Hollywood, and that white sands and cliffs were no more predominant in *The Lone Ranger* than in their other Westerns of the period.

If these introductory reminiscences are essentially personal rather than critical, it is to emphasize that almost *all* appreciation of the serial has to be largely personal, and based to a very great degree on one's age at the time and the conditions under which one saw it. Moreover, the serial is a branch of film unique and exclusive unto itself, and has to be judged and regarded accordingly. Mr. Barbour is generous with his use of such words as "classic," "masterpiece" and "superb"—and within the confines of his text, he is quite justified. By serial standards, a film like *The Adventures of Captain Marvel is* a masterpiece; the juxtaposition of the best serials of Republic (for example, *Mysterious Dr. Satan* or *Drums of Fu Manchu*) next to the worst of the independents (*Custer's Last Stand* or *The Black Coin*) automatically makes "classics" of the Republics. A bravura performance by Lionel Atwill or Eduardo Ciannelli as a Republic villain certainly is "superb" acting compared with the listless and thoughtless reading of lines by a Jack Ingram or a Gene Stutenroth in a Columbia serial. But everything in film is relative: to term a serial a "masterpiece" is in no way to imply that it can stand side by side with such genuine film masterpieces as *Sunrise, Intolerance,* or *Citizen Kane.* There are perhaps only a handful of true film masterpieces which can hold their own as independent works of art with the other great masterpieces of the art world: painting, sculpture, poetry, music. There is no film serial (or at least, no *American* serial) which can call itself a masterpiece outside of its own little world. With full regard for the skill of the serials, the money they made, and the entertainment they brought to millions, the serials have not added one iota of development

to either the art or the history of the film. One could sweep them all away, blot them out totally, and the blow to film history would not be a major one. Indeed, if the serial had never evolved at all, it is unlikely that the course of film would have been changed or diverted in any way.

This may seem like a very harsh judgment, especially from one who is an admitted devotee of the serial. Obviously one can't just sweep away four full decades of serials—some 3,000 hours of film—nor do I wish to. But unlike the two-reel comedy or even the B-Western, the serial was never innovational. Everything it had, everything it did, represented a kind of brain-picking from what had gone before. The best serials were the ones made by the directors who loved their craft, loved film—and had seen a lot of it. They knew what had been done before, and how best to adapt it to their own work. The most common element of all serials was the steady building of suspense to climaxes via speed, action and, cross-cutting—devices that D. W. Griffith had explored in his Biograph shorts of 1908–1913 and had brought to fruition in *The Birth of a Nation* and *Intolerance* in the mid-teens, just as the serials were getting under way. Serial directors, who would be the last to call themselves artists, probably knew more about the true art of film than many a more pretentious and acclaimed director of features. How else can one explain the frequent references to classic silent work that one finds scattered throughout the best of even the talkie serials? *Flash Gordon* (1936) uses designs and prop-machines in its "atom furnace" set that obviously derive from Fritz Lang's *Metropolis* of a decade earlier. Their presence is not vital to either set or story-line, but it is one of those intangible assets that makes all the difference between a good serial and a mediocre one. Another more striking example is provided by *Undersea Kingdom,* a serial of the same period. On a smaller scale, of course, one battle sequence is based exactly on the monumental battle in 1916's *Intolerance,* complete to such details as the destruction of the scaling towers and the utilization of a fanciful flame-thrower.

In view of the structure of the serial and the nature of its production methods, it is not surprising that its makers have pursued ingenuity rather than creativity. The director of a B-Western has probably more "artistic freedom" than any other director in the world. His product isn't important enough to warrant front-office supervision, nor does anybody care very much if he deviates from his script. Moreover, much of the time he is away from the studio—either on location, or at the studio ranch—away from even nominal interference. As long as he brings in a salable product, on time and under budget, nobody is going to care whether he delivers five reels of action or a five-reel masterpiece. Admittedly, shooting has to be fast, and the average director is more interested in shaving time off an already tight schedule than in exploring the niceties of camera composition or shooting a scene so that it is, in a sense, edited in the camera. Yet a director who really cares, and who has ambitions beyond B pictures, will take precisely that care. A case in point is Joseph H. Lewis, who directed some of the best of the Bob Baker and Johnny Mack Brown Westerns for Universal before going on to big-budget thrillers. The style and finesse that he brought to films like *Courage of the West* and *Arizona Cyclone* really paid off and lifted them well above formula level. It's unlikely that his efforts increased their box-office yield in any way, but at least he had the personal satisfaction of seeing a one-hour film in which his style was consistent and recognizable, and also, probably, the more commercial satisfaction of knowing that a film that good might well attract the attention of production higher-ups who could promote him to bigger and better properties.

No such incentives exist with the serial, nor would they be practical to pursue if they did. By its very nature, the serial is mechanically constructed to fit a set pattern, a set running time, and a set audience. Given a rudimentary story-line, it has to be developed to encompass as much action as possible, to avoid dramatic entanglements which entail careful writing and acting, and to utilize such budget-paring ingredients as stock footage and standing sets as frequently as possible. Moreover, because of the great length of footage involved—some five hours per average complete serial—and the frequent re-utilization of the same key sets and locations, production is always broken down mathematically so that all the shots involving a given set or a key player are filmed at the same time. Further, two (and often more) directors are usually involved in the average serial, one handling action scenes, particularly fights, another directing the purely dialogue sequences, and perhaps a third doing the second-unit location work (car chases, Indian–cavalry encounters, and so forth). As a result, no one director exercises total control over a serial or is able to impose a definite style. (Admittedly, two directors working together as a team could, in time, evolve a kind of style—and some did.) In addition, with production at such breakneck speed, the kind of niceties that Joseph Lewis could afford in a humble Western were sheer luxuries in a serial; moreover, they would be wasted, since an adroit piece of editing or careful attention paid to the way an actor handled his lines would just be lost in such a morass of footage. Audiences wouldn't remember little moments of artistic endeavor—and unless they were spotted within the first couple of chapters, the chances were that studio executives would never get to see them at all. So the shrewd serial director aimed not so much at artistry as at gimmickry, at making his serial look far more expensive than it was, dreaming up original little bits of business that could make his audience sit up and take notice because they were getting something new—and all this, if possible, without any increase in budget or shooting time. A typical example is provided by a Universal serial of the mid-thirties, *Scouts to the Rescue*, in which a lost tribe of Indians was given a most impressive and undecipherable guttural language. Certainly the gimmick worked on me as a child, and it wasn't until years later, when I ran off a print on a projector that also worked in reverse, that I tumbled to the trick. The Indians spoke perfectly normal dialogue—which was then printed in reverse. Very often they were physically motionless, so that the *picture* could be printed in reverse too, and a perfect lip-synch maintained!

None of this is meant to imply that there was no artistry in the serial: there *was*, but it was all devoted to areas where it really counted (and could be reused!), and again, it was merely an extension of techniques and styles that existed outside the serials. Republic, for example, lavished great care on their miniatures; they were often incredibly realistic, putting to shame a lot of the miniature work in million-dollar specials. The miniatures in MGM's sound *Ben Hur* are positively amateurish compared with the work done by the Lydecker brothers for Republic. There is artistry too in the choreography (and the word is used here deliberately) of fight scenes, and in the slick utilization of running inserts in chase scenes. But it is a kind of mechanical artistry, honed to perfection through years of polishing, nonetheless exciting for being so efficiently manufactured, but still mechanical.

It's significant, I think, that while many major directors emerged from the ranks of two-reel comedies and Westerns (among them Charlie Chaplin, Buster Keaton, Mal St. Clair, Frank Capra, John Ford, William Wyler), graduates from the serial were far less impressive. Only two really major directorial names got their start in serials, George Marshall and W. S. Van Dyke, and even Van Dyke had had an apprenticeship with Griffith prior to his serials. Both Marshall and Van Dyke learned how to keep their pictures constantly on the move, and how to bring their films in on time and under budget —a particularly useful lesson for Van Dyke, who made his best pictures at MGM in the thirties, where the prevailing *modus operandi* was to shoot slowly and to retake (or remake) as much as necessary. His lightning methods made him the envy of other directors, the delight of the budget-conscious front-office, and, sadly, an object of genial derision by most critics who couldn't believe—*Trader Horn, White Shadows in the South Seas,* and *The Thin Man* notwithstanding—that pictures made quickly, and by an ex-serial director, could be any good! Most directors who proved adept at serial-making—Ray Taylor, Ford Beebe, Spencer Gordon Bennet—tended to stay with the genre throughout their careers. And, too, the serial proved a useful haven for once-leading directors (primarily of action material) who, in their later days, found themselves short on good assignments: Lambert Hillyer, Elmer Clifton, James Horne. Writing for serials is such a specialized field that relatively few of its scenarists ever left it; none certainly made any major marks in movies outside of the chapter-play area. Even the number of stars who were discovered in the serial is few: Warren William, George Brent, Jennifer Jones, Carole Landis. (John Wayne was a minor but established player well before his three early sound serials). As with the directors, however, the serial was a welcome refuge for many of the veteran stars who were having problems finding suitable roles but whose names still meant something to the patrons of serials—Herbert Rawlinson, Hoot Gibson, Francis X. Bushman, Clara Kimball Young, Kenneth Harlan.

On the whole, however, actors were always somewhat handicapped by the production methods of the serial, and they rarely had a chance to perform at their best. Most of the straight dramatic scenes were shot even more out of context than is usual in films, and the actors—especially the bit-players—rarely knew to what set of circumstances they were reacting, or into what context their scenes would be cut. Many supporting "roles," not accounted for in the script, would be created on the spot to provide instant justification or explanation for a situation and the actor would usually be a bit-player doing half-a-dozen other "roles" in the serial, sometimes with just a moustache or a pair of spectacles to "disguise" him, and often not even that. There was rarely time to establish any real kind of characterization, let alone the "motivation" so beloved by method actors. Of course, the action star personalities—Ralph Byrd, Buster Crabbe, Kane Richmond—had little trouble breezing through their familiar roles in dashing style. Not so successful were the less experienced, off-beat actors, who were often used by Republic in many of their leads partly because they worked at cheaper rates, and partly because their somewhat nondescript appearance made the matter of doubling easier. Such players as Robert Wilcox, Walter Reed, and Harry Lauter were far too dour and colorless to be a consistent match with the dashing image created by their doubles for the action scenes. For sheer lethargy and absence of get-up-and-go, however, some prize should surely be awarded to Ralph Graves for his performance as the G–man hero of the singularly dull *The Black Coin.* Not once did Graves (normally quite a good and pleasing actor) seem to snap out of his sleepy-eyed coma, and the apex of his inertia was reached in an early chapter when he looked out of the window of his plane (safely on the ground) to note that one wing and a fuel tank were merrily blazing away. "The plane's on fire" he remarked in a conversational tone of total disinterest, lazily forcing himself to rise from his seat as though in doubt whether to leave or not!

In contrast to his nonchalant "cool," the casts of Columbia serials were rushed about from situation to situation in a state of perpetual frenzy. It seemed almost a matter of policy to keep the players in such a state of non-stop motion that neither they nor the audience had time to stop and think about the absurdity of it all. This hectic activity was by no means limited to the fight scenes, where such stalwarts as Warren Hull (*The Spider's Web*) or Jack Holt (*Holt of the Secret Service*) would cheerfully take on (and vanquish) half a dozen heavies in fights of Keystone Cop speed and animation, but also to simple dramatic or transitional scenes. Nobody ever walked from a cabin to a car in a Columbia serial, they *ran*— and when they reached their destination they tumbled out like the Marx Brothers in the stateroom sequence of *A Night at the Opera,* and started running again. This breathless lack of decorum was inflicted on leading ladies and dignified character actors as well as mere hoodlums, and was emphasized by undercranked camerawork which gave their haste an even more frenzied appearance—to say nothing of the furious *agitato* music (usually by Lee Zahler) which helped to speed them on their way. Under such circumstances, subtlety in acting was an impossibility: players had neither the time (nor, probably, the breath) to deliver lines with care or respect, and simply had to hurl them out before being whisked off to something else. Small wonder that even the simplest line of dialogue seemed to be delivered amateurishly, with all the emphases on the wrong words. In fairness to Columbia, however, it would seem that this deliberate stress on artificial speed was part of an overall scheme to "camp" up their serials long before that absurd, much-abused (and happily now dying) term came into common usage. Although the studio made a handful of good early ones, Columbia rapidly lost interest in turning out quality serials, abandoning both the superior production values and action content of the contemporary Republic serials and the more reasonable and logical story values of the Universals. The Columbia serials directed by James Horne were clearly tongue-in-cheek, with exaggerated melodramatic gestures, derisive and sarcastic end-of-chapter narrations, and moments of truly lunatic comedy involving the villains. Serial purists understandably resented this and have never liked Horne's serials. Yet he was too good a director, too much a past master of great silent

and sound comedy (*The Cruise of the Jasper B,* Laurel and Hardy's *Big Business*) not to know precisely what he was doing. Undoubtedly he reasoned that to play the scripts straight, with their stereotyped stories and meager budgets, could only result in serials spectacularly inferior to the competitive ones issued by Republic and Universal. Playing them for comedy didn't make them better, but it did keep them lively, distinctive, and different. Their speed and constant changes of pace, however, and their intermingling of melodrama and farce, to say nothing of their frequent elements of what we would now call black comedy, made them even more of a challenge for actors, who could do nothing but go along for the ride. For the most part, the actors who fared best in serials (and *not* in Columbia serials, let it be added) were the well-established character actors (Irving Pichel, Ralph Morgan) and the bravura villains (Bela Lugosi, Lionel Atwill, Eduardo Ciannelli), players who had the expertise to go through their familiar paces with polish and aplomb, utilizing every bit of business at their disposal, employing every nuance of expression and delivery to build and magnify the quality of what they had to work with. Polished and suave villains like Atwill even managed to get away with audience-acceptance of that oldest and silliest of serial clichés, the villain's foolhardy reluctance to dispose of the hero while he has him in his power. After episodes of the most elaborate (and expensive) attempts to have the hero blown up, incinerated, guillotined, or eaten by crocodiles, there always arrives a moment when the hapless hero has pulled a boner and lies unconscious at the feet of his enemy. One of the smarter and more farsighted hoodlums aims a gun point-blank at his head. "Don't waste a bullet on him!" admonishes the mastermind, preferring to leave the hero's disposal to the mechanical contrivance which forms that week's chapter title—and chapter ending. Needless to say, such a priceless opportunity rarely arises again—or if it does it is similarly muffed for the sake of self-indulgent sadism!

Perhaps the least sung of all serial heroes is the editor: not only was he responsible for putting the mass of repetitious footage together, and creating as exciting a tempo as possible, but in many cases he had to salvage the mistakes or omissions of directors who, working at top speed, might understandably have left out minor scenes or found it impractical to go back to reshoot scenes that turned out badly. With very little to work with, for serial budgets didn't allow for the luxury of protection shots or standby footage, the editor often performed near-miracles. The salvage work might be apparent, but the show went on! Universal, always a little more concerned with story values than with action for its own sake, often neglected in the script stage to plant sufficient motivation or explanation in the dialogue. As a result, the end product often looked much like the extension of a comic strip, action flowing too facilely from point A to point C without the intermediate justification or logical explanation at point B. *Flash Gordon,* with its welter of scientific gimmickry, was especially guilty of this, and since the film was a major serial in its day, designed for more than just the kiddie trade, it obviously bothered Universal production heads. The solution was to dub in quick, pithy lines all the way through—a masterly compression of scientific data into one sentence here to explain a complicated bit of rocketship wizardry, or an expository line there to justify everybody's knowing exactly what to do without having to discuss it first. Unfortunately, the same deep booming voice was used for these lines (an average of four or five such lines appeared in each episode) throughout the entire serial. Whether it was the villainous Ming, the heroic Prince Barin, or the enterprising Dr. Zarkov who was supposed to be speaking, the voice was always the same—and the unintended result was the seeming omnipresence of a benign Deity, forever booming out instructions and helpful advice at the frequent moments of crisis!

There was usually little that the editor could do to bolster belief in the solutions to the previous week's climaxes: either they tended to be too cut-and-dried and formularized to be really exciting, or they cheated outrageously, banking rather forlornly on the audience's faulty memory. An example that comes readily to mind is a giant ore-crusher falling *on* Bob Livingston's chest in *The Vigilantes Are Coming,* the hero groaning in agony at the fadeout—but the following week he manages to remove himself from harm's way in ample time. Similarly, in *Winners of the West* Dick Foran lies unconscious in the path of an onrushing locomotive which thunders *over* his inert form at the end of one episode,

while in the next he staggers to his feet and wanders away while the train is still a good hundred yards down the track! Once in a while serials were so haphazardly shot that *no* "rescue" footage was delivered at all; thus, Johnny Mack Brown came to the end of one episode of *The Oregon Trail* under a herd of stampeding horses. Nothing was shot to save him from his predicament, so the editor had simply to ignore the whole thing and start the following chapter as though nothing had happened. Such lack of logic was, unfortunately, too often a hallmark of the American serial. The early chapters of *The Secret of Treasure Island* made a great to-do about a pirate's ghost, a lively skeleton that, among other enterprising activities, engaged the hero in a sword-fight or two. He was conveniently dropped several chapters before the end, and then explained away in the fifteenth episode as merely an image thrown by a projector! Even a first-class editor was comparatively helpless against such odds.

Another obstacle—particularly at Universal—was the musical director's apparent unwillingness to see the film he was scoring! For the most part *Flash Gordon* is a well-edited serial, but many of its highlights are lessened by the too-casual application of stock music and themes from earlier films. A pastorale theme may drone on through an exciting fight scene, while potentially gripping episodes of transitions from suspense to action are let down by musical scoring which does not punctuate those changes in mood. Perhaps all of these rather petty criticisms fall under the general heading of a lack of showmanship. Given that the serial is an unambitious branch of the art, geared to a set pattern with predictable costs and returns, too many directors forget that a basically juvenile audience follows a serial with loyalty and respect. Showmanship, sadly, has been too often limited to the opening three chapters, which are the ones shown to the trade for review purposes and to get bookings. A disproportionate amount of the budget usually goes to these opening chapters, along with the more imaginative elements of the plot too. Tom Mix's *The Miracle Rider* offered all sorts of elaborate gimmicks, some of a semi-science-fiction nature, in its first few episodes; thereafter both the gimmicks and often Mr. Mix too were conspicuous by their absence. Strong plot-lines, too, have a habit of dissolving after they have been established at the very beginning. Columbia serials were notorious for bogging down in single situations which never developed, and thus they were merely a loosely connected string of fights and chases. Worst of all were the "tug-of-war" plots as exemplified by the Buck Jones serial *The Roaring West,* in which practically the entire continuity was devoted to an old prospector and his map: they were captured by the badmen, rescued, captured by Indians, rescued; then his daughter was captured by badmen, he went to the rescue and was recaptured—ad infinitum, all against the background of a wagon train that lumbered from nowhere to nowhere, much like the plot itself.

Most inexcusable of all of course was the betraying of juvenile loyalty by coming up with a last chapter which shunned spectacular action in favor of wrapping it all up as economically as possible. The studios saw no point in ladling out largesse for a climactic episode, yet audiences who had been following the serial faithfully for fifteen weeks had a right to feel cheated when the unspeakable villain was brought to book without a chase or a fight. While certainly some studios did finish up their serials with a bang and/or imaginative twists in the ultimate unmasking of the villain, too many took the easier and less exciting path.

The history of the American serial is a frustrating one of missed opportunities, perhaps because of its own self-imposed limitations. Even in the earlier silent days, when the serial enjoyed its biggest box-office boom and was designed for adult approval, it stuck rigidly to the two-reel format. The Europeans on the other hand, respected the serial tradition and developed it with care and imagination, giving it the kind of running time and story sense that they thought it warranted. The German serials of Fritz Lang and Joe May had wildly extravagant—and romantic—plot-lines, and the episodes (which were complete in themselves, yet ended on the thresholds of obviously greater adventures) often ran for more than an hour. Moreover, they were totally unformula in concept and thoroughly unpredictable: one episode of Joe May's *Mistress of the World* suddenly turned itself into a kind of Lubitsch self-satire, playing entirely for comedy, at the same time establishing the fact that more traditional adventure fare was forthcoming the following week. And the early

French serials of Louis Feuillade are unreservedly film classics. His *Les Vampires,* constructed more like a feature than a serial, spends almost two of its seven hours in relatively tame establishment of characters and plot, then follows with a dizzy succession of thrills and sensations that mount to a fantastic crescendo. *Les Vampires* has thrill upon thrill, but it also presents fascinating character and story development, plus real beauty, poetry, and an odd intermingling of documentary values with surrealism. Even today, well over half a century after it was made, it stands as a model of what the serial should be—and what it could have been in this country. But Hollywood was developing so quickly in the years before the twenties: so many great directors—Griffith, Tourneur, Ford, Chaplin, von Stroheim—were maturing so rapidly, understandably bypassing the humble serial in favor of more challenging technical and story innovations. Apart from Abel Gance, a director whose genius rivaled Griffith's, the comedian Max Linder, France could muster few names in the 1910–1920 period (the great Méliès, of course, belonged to the earlier decade) to match the staggering outpouring of creative talent from Hollywood in those formulative years. So we can afford to be generous to France and acknowledge that Feuillade and his masterly serials led the field then—and still do.

Yet while the American serial was entertaining us and bringing healthy profits to its promoters, it was also performing several other valuable if unwitting sociological and historical functions. First of all, the serial always depended on speed —speed that was as up to the minute as possible— which meant a maximum reliance on automobiles and locomotives at first, and later on speedboats, racing cars, and airplanes. Since it was economically desirable to shoot out of doors as much as possible, and since, too, these props demanded it, many serials (particularly in the silent period) stressed a maximum of location shooting on busy city streets and country roads, thus capturing on film an invaluable record of a changing America as it was emerging into a rapidly more automated age. And since serials were so concerned with a direct confrontation between good and evil, they were always careful to spell out the moral standards of the day; to later generations these unintended and therefore quite honest depictions of the moral, racial, sexual, and other climates of their day can be both revealing and valuable. The casual acceptance of interracial humor and homosexuality (Ben Wilson serials made a genial running gag out of transvestism in the mid-twenties) reminds us how less hot and bothered we all got in those days about facets of everyday life that are now considered controversial. And although *Flash Gordon* seems to encourage a healthy interest in sex—the fetchingly underclad Dale Arden (Jean Rogers) is energetically pursued by a number of outer-space lechers, ranging from the winged King Vultan to the arch-fiend Ming himself—the script makes it quite plain that an unmarried male hero must be ignorant of such matters. Buster Crabbe as Flash seems naïvely unaware of Princess Aura's carnal interest in him as she runs her fingers over his rippling muscles; and when Flash and Dale are the guests of a lesser interplanetary ruler, he sends them to their retirement with the rather pointed remark, "Take them to their *separate* quarters!" (Universal seemed especially anxious to assure audiences of the total morality not only of heroes and heroines but even of complete crowds; who can forget burgomaster E. E. Clive dismissing a huge mob in *The Bride of Frankenstein* with the admonition, "It's high time every decent man *and wife* was home in bed"?) *Flash Gordon* offered a further contemporary reference: although the decidedly unroyal decor in Ming's palace was an odd combination of old and new—ray guns juxtaposed with Roman swords and armor, a rather tatty fur rug flung on the floor before the imposing altar-like throne—it was an Oriental motif that dominated. Sculptures of dragons, Ming's

tapering fingernails, his long thin moustache, his kimono-like robes, all of these were reminders that the personification of satanic evil was still to a degree associated with the only slowly disappearing image of the "yellow peril."

In the past, serials have served as a useful training ground for directors and stars, and through them valuable lessons in production economy have been learned and applied in the mainstream of film production. In the present, the now-defunct film serial has come to be regarded (with condescension by some, overawe by others) as a definite and acceptable kind of pop-art culture, so much so that on the open black market a print of *Flash Gordon* or *Captain America* will fetch more than an *Intolerance* or a *Citizen Kane!* In the future, as well as serving as a kind of signpost to contemporary tastes and mores, the American film serial may well find acceptance as a serious branch of American film art. If this seems unlikely, just recall how long it took for the Western—or for the comedies of Laurel and Hardy—to be afforded the respect they deserve.

These notes, written with fondness and genuine affection for the genre, *are* written "looking back," and thus carry the perspective and perhaps reluctant realism that has to come with time. As you read through Mr. Barbour's recapitulation of the serials, however, I suggest that you don't "look back," but instead try to see them with the eyes of youth, as we saw them in those less complicated and certainly more innocent days—when the serials were as guileless and perfect and free of flaw and blemish as we were ourselves!

WILLIAM K. EVERSON

DAYS OF THRILLS AND ADVENTURE

Pearl White, the most famous of all serial heroines, in a 1918 portrait.

1. The First Episode

WHILE THIS VOLUME deals almost entirely with the sound serial, I should, nevertheless, devote some space, however slight, to explaining the origin of the format in its embryonic stages.

Mention the silent serial and the name that automatically comes to mind is that of Pearl White. Somehow Pearl, with her singularly daring exploits in *The Perils of Pauline,* has managed to overshadow the stars of more than two hundred and fifty serials produced during the eighteen years between 1913 and 1930 to the point where most people are hard put to name *any* other star of that period.

However famous Pearl White may have become, she was not the first serial queen. That honor belongs to two long-since-forgotten screen heroines, Mary Fuller and Kathlyn Williams.

The serial format was one of the last experiments to be tried in those early days of film-making. William K. Everson, one of the most knowledgeable film historians in the United States, explained the birth of the new form superbly in the first issue of *Screen Facts Magazine,* published in 1963:

Curiously, the serials were late in reaching the screen. By 1913, when the first one was tried out, almost everything else had already been done. There were established, or rapidly-forming, filmic traditions in melodrama, Westerns and comedy. 1912 had seen the feature film (of five and six reels) accepted as normal; there had been experiments in wide-screen, color and even in sound. And like sound and wide-screen, the serials came in initially as a gimmick. They were tied in with newspaper serials, the idea being that the film would boost newspaper circulation, and the newspaper-readers would flock to see their linotype heroes and heroines come alive in celluloid. It was a good stunt and it worked.

The first tie-in between the screen and the printed page was *What Happened to Mary?,* released by the Edison Company in 1912. Unlike the serials we remember so fondly with their cliff-hanger endings, the first serial more closely resembled a television series, with each episode telling a completely resolved story within its relatively short running time. Of course the events that happened to Mary Fuller were pretty tame compared with what Pearl White had to go through only two years later, but it *was* a beginning. One episode climaxed with poor Mary escaping the villains by tying bedsheets together, climbing down from a window, and running to join the Salvation Army!

The pace picked up considerably a year later when Kathlyn Williams starred in an exciting jungle serial called *The Adventures of Kathlyn,* and 1914 brought *The Perils of Pauline.* The basic story running through the twenty self-contained episodes of this most famous of all silent serials was relatively simple. The villains, headed by Paul Panzer, were trying to kill Pauline in order to gain her inheritance. The adventures found the principals traveling all over the world trying everything from time-bombs to murder by snakebite to get rid of the plucky heroine, but Pauline survived every delicious intrigue and danger. Following on the heels of this tremendous film success, Pearl starred in *The Exploits of Elaine,* which ran for thirty-six episodes and found our heroine matching wits against the mysterious Clutching Hand, a power-mad demon bent on world domination. Pearl continued to thrill audiences in subsequent better-made, but less famous, serials like *The Lightning Raider, The Iron Claw,* and *The Black Secret,* among others.

But Pearl's cinema success was not to go unchallenged by other attractive screen lovelies who felt they could match, if not exceed, the exploits of the reigning serial queen. Helen Holmes gained a noteworthy reputation for her action-packed train sequences in films like *The Hazards of Helen* and *A Lass of the Lumberlands,* and Ruth Roland gave Pearl a run for her crown when she thrilled audiences in *Ruth of the Range, The Avenging Arrow, White Eagle,* and others. And there were many others: Eileen Sedgwick, Arline Pretty, Grace Cunard, Neva Gerber—girls who thrilled millions, but never gained the fame attached to Pearl White.

And the men? There were so many of them, such as Joe Bonomo, Ben Wilson, Crane Wilbur, Herbert Rawlinson, Eddie Polo, Jack Mulhall, Jack Mower, Charles Hutchinson, Elmo Lincoln, Francis Ford, William Duncan, and William Desmond.

And, on rare occasions, the serials would pair two performers whose screen magnetism had audiences begging for more joint appearances. Such was the case with pert Allene Ray and stunt man-actor Walter Miller, each of whom had made numerous serials on his own or teamed with others. Films like *Play Ball, The Black Book, Snowed In,* and *Sunken Silver* showed the couple at their exciting best.

Once in a great while the serials were able to attract celebrity stars. Harry Houdini appeared as the lead in *The Master Mystery* in 1919, but the film was not an overwhelming success, even though the master escape-artist did provide numerous thrilling trick escapes. Much more successful was the appearance of Jack Dempsey, the famous heavyweight boxing champ, in 1920's *Daredevil Jack.*

Because sound had not yet entered into serial production, the stress had to be on visual action; thus the real stars of the silent serials were those who could perform most of their own stunts. This accounted for the tremendous success of men like Walter Miller and Joe Bonomo in the twenties, as it had accounted for similar success of the ladies in the previous decade.

And if the great serial stars on the screen garnered all the fame and attention, no less credit should be given to the men behind the camera who helped them earn it, men like Frank Leon Smith, who turned out screenplay after screenplay (*Snowed In, The Green Archer,* etc.), incorporating new and thrilling escapades in each to amaze and entertain a serial-hungry public, and Spencer Gordon Bennet, the king of the serial directors, whose total output is deserving of a book in itself (he directed the final sound serial made in 1956). They are truly two remarkable men in serial history.

But all good things, as the saying goes, must come to an end, and so it was with the silent serial. By the end of the twenties interest in serials had waned considerably. Perhaps it was over-saturation. After all, nearly three hundred productions in eighteen years provided more than just a casual amount of movie excitement. Or, perhaps, audiences living in that wild era of the twenties found their screen heroes less heroic than the real-life heroes who made headlines daily as they waged war against real rather than "reel" gangsters. The serials still had an audience, even if it was limited, and the coming of sound really didn't increase its size by much. The Depression of the early thirties took care of that. It wasn't until the middle thirties that the serials once again found overflow crowds cramming their local theatres to see a new type of screen hero—Buster Crabbe as *Flash Gordon.* A new golden age of the serial had begun.

Pearl White and Buster Crabbe. The mention of their names conjured up visions of a Saturday-afternoon world that no longer exists, except in our fondest memories—that wonderful world of the serial.

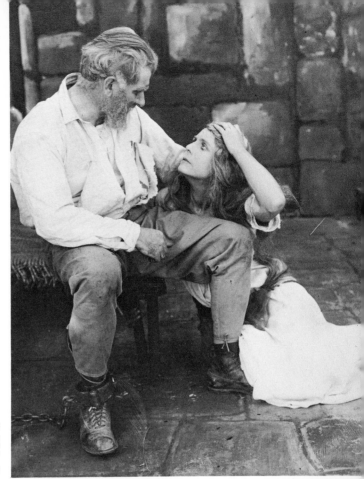

right: Lafayette McKee and Kathlyn Williams in the first true serial, *The Adventures of Kathlyn* (Selig 1913). *below:* Pearl White is about to be rudely awakened by the Clutching Hand in *The Exploits of Elaine* (Pathé 1914).

right: Ruth Roland, another popular favorite, gets the drop on a typical Oriental menace in *The Adventures of Ruth* (Pathé 1919). *below:* Pearl White seems to have her hands full in this scene from *Plunder* (Pathé 1923).

Helen Holmes' spectacular railroad heroics made her rank as a top serial queen in films like *The Hazards of Helen* (Kalem 1914).

above: Truman Van Dyke was the athletic hero of *The Jungle Goddess* (Export-Import 1922). *left:* Walter Miller and Ethlyne Clair are about to unmask the mysterious Wolf-Devil in *Queen of the Northwoods* (Pathé 1929).

above: That's Lionel Barrymore glowering at Pearl White while another mystery man listens in *The Romance of Elaine* (Pathé 1915).

below: Howard Estabrook is trapped by a secret society in *The Mysteries of Myra* (Pathé-International 1916).

above: Frank Lackteen, one of the most famous of all serial villains, obviously has plans for Allene Ray in *Hawk of the Hills* (Pathé 1927). *left:* Gladys McConnell gets an unhelping hand in *The Tiger's Shadow* (Pathé 1928). *below:* The most famous serial team of the twenties was **Allene Ray** and Walter Miller, here trying to solve the mystery of *The Black Book* (Pathé 1929).

Heavyweight champion of the world Jack Dempsey in his serial appearance as *Daredevil Jack* (Pathé 1920).

Onslow Stevens seems at a distinct disadvantage in *The Vanishing Shadow* (Universal 1934).

2. The Early-Talkie and Independent Serials

ALTHOUGH SEVERAL INDEPENDENT PRODUCERS tried to invade the serial territory dominated by Mascot and Universal in the early and mid-thirties, their efforts, on the whole, were most unsatisfactory. They simply did not have the financial resources to do an adequate job, and the cheapness of their production was only too evident to the audiences who had come to expect much more in their Saturday cinema adventures.

RKO's solo entry in the field was *The Last Frontier,* an utterly pedestrian Western in which Lon Chaney, Jr., portrayed a pseudo-Zorro avenging victimized frontiersmen. Weiss Productions turned out two mildly entertaining thrillers, *The Clutching Hand* and *The Broken Coin.* The former had silent leading man Jack Mulhall playing Craig Kennedy, a famous fictional detective, on the trail of a ruthless band of kidnappers headed by the Clutching Hand who were trying to acquire a secret formula for making synthetic gold; the latter featured Ralph Graves and Dave O'Brien, who were searching for secret papers believed to contain information that could be of value in trapping smugglers. Many background sets utilized in *The Clutching Hand* were re-used in *The Broken Coin.* Another long and tedious affair was the Weiss production of *Custer's Last Stand*, which, the advertising proudly proclaimed, was actually "based on historical events leading up to Custer's Last Fight."

Rex Lease led an enormous cast through the fifteen seemingly endless episodes.

One of the more interesting independents was the Edgar Rice Burroughs-produced *The New Adventures of Tarzan.* Starring Herman Brix (later known as Bruce Bennett) as the famous ape man, the film was photographed on location in the jungles of Guatemala. The story found Tarzan joining an expedition trying to locate the fabulous Green Goddess, a priceless Mayan relic containing a fortune in rare gems. Brix was an ideal choice to play the strenuous role. Buster Crabbe had been less successful in portraying the same character in *Tarzan, the Fearless* two years earlier in 1933. Released through Principal Pictures, this adventure of the legendary jungle lord found him searching for co-star Jacqueline Wells' father, who was studying ancient tribes and had been captured by the mysterious people of Zar, God of the Emerald Fingers, headed by Mischa Auer playing an evil high priest. *The New Adventures of Tarzan* was edited into two feature versions which frequently played double-feature houses in the forties and early fifties, and a feature version of *Tarzan, the Fearless* is included in the current television package of Tarzan films.

Another favorite independent serial was *Return of Chandu,* also re-edited and released in two feature versions by Principal Pictures. With

Bela Lugosi in the title role, the chapter play was a delight on every count as the master magician fought against a secret cult of idol worshipers.

While the independents fought a valiant fight to attract box-office attention, Universal was turning out exciting action fare on its own. Richard Talmadge, that stunt ace of the twenties and thirties, finally got his own starring serial, *Pirate Treasure*, and filled it full of his own personal brand of screen heroics. Onslow Stevens managed to oppose a really antagonistic robot and persevere in *The Vanishing Shadow;* Frank Albertson dared a thousand thrills aboard *The Lost Special;* Evalyn Knapp tried to bring back *The Perils of Pauline* with dismal results; Tim McCoy fought Indians in the first talking serial, *The Indians Are Coming*, and arsonists in *Heroes of the Flames;* and Tom Tyler took turns hunting in the jungle in *Jungle Mystery*, riding in the North Country in *Clancy of the Mounted*, and flying through the air in *Phantom of the Air*. More than a dozen other heroes helped the years pass quickly until the most famous hero of them all emerged from the studio—*Flash Gordon!*

Not to be outdone by Universal, Mascot Pictures managed to turn out a number of fine serials starring some of the most popular screen heroes of the day, and some who rose to spectacular fame in later years.

John Wayne starred in three popular serials produced by the company. *Shadow of the Eagle* found him battling a mystery man known only as the Eagle who was out to wreak vengeance on several men he suspected of cheating him. When the script called for a plane to sky-write a message from the Eagle the miniature used was so toylike that it was hard to watch the sequence without breaking up with laughter. In *Hurricane Express*, big John was battling the mysterious Wrecker who was doing his best to wreck everything in sight, including John. The final film in the trilogy, *The Three Musketeers*, had him helping Jack Mulhall, Raymond Hatton, and Francis X. Bushman, Jr., uncover the mysterious El Shaitan.

Mystery Squadron found cowboy star Bob Steele temporarily hanging up his guns and spurs long enough to uncover the mysterious Black Ace in an exciting aerial thriller, and

Burn 'Em Up Barnes had Jack Mulhall and Frankie Darro fighting a gang of racketeers bent on taking over their transportation business.

One of the really superb films in the series was Mascot's 1935 *The Fighting Marines*, featuring Grant Withers and Adrian Morris (brother of Chester Morris). The thrilling plot had the two men battling a mysterious enemy known only as the Tiger Shark. The Shark operated from a remote island and traveled by means of a huge flying "wing," later re-used by Republic in *Dick Tracy* when Mascot merged into the new Republic Pictures Corporation.

Other popular Mascot favorites were *Phantom Empire*, which brought stardom to its singing cowboy star, Gene Autry; *The Last of the Mohicans*, with Harry Carey in a very loosely based version of the James Fenimore Cooper story; *The Whispering Shadow*, with Bela Lugosi slinking around in his best Dracula-like fashion, and which had a thrilling climax to its first chapter featuring a miniature autogiro; *Mystery Mountain*, with cowboy star Ken Maynard taking twelve episodes to discover the Rattler when we knew the truth in chapter one; *The Miracle Rider*, featuring Tom Mix in his only starring serial, and his final film; *The Galloping Ghost*, with football hero Red Grange chasing bad men instead of pigskin; *Fighting with Kit Carson*, featuring Johnny Mack Brown in the first of his five starring Western serials; and the Rin-Tin-Tin, Jr., epics, *The Wolf Dog, Adventures of Rex and Rinty, Lightning Warrior* (ably assisted by future star George Brent), and *The Lone Defender*.

If there was a common flaw in most of these early serials, it was a lack of pacing. They all seemed to drag on interminably, and even chase sequences, which should have been thrilling, were stretched beyond normal patience. Adding to the problem was an almost complete absence of background music. Even the dullest possible serial can be tolerated if an accompanying musical score is sufficiently interesting, but the only music in these early vehicles was played behind the opening credits. But, for all their faults, a re-viewing of many of them still finds us enjoying them for what they were.

And the golden age of the serial was just about to begin!

above: Bela Lugosi seems to be getting the upper hand against Herman Brix (later Bruce Bennett) in *Shadow of Chinatown* (Victory 1936). *below:* Herbert Rawlinson as Blake helps assistant, Ralph Byrd, in *Blake of Scotland Yard* (Victory 1937).

left: Grant Withers and Adrian Morris were excellent in *The Fighting Marines* (Mascot 1935). This serial had all the superb ingredients that became Republic's trademark when Mascot merged into the new Republic Pictures Corp. *below:* Bela Lugosi is up to something mysterious, as usual, in *The Whispering Shadow* (Mascot 1933).

above: George Brent was one of the few major stars who appeared in early serials. That's Rin-Tin-Tin watching Bob Kortman cover Brent in *Lightning Warrior* (Mascot 1931). *left:* Frankie Darro is about to take care of Bob Kortman who was about to take care of Jack Mulhall in *Burn 'Em Up Barnes* (Mascot 1934).

right: Lucile Browne and James Flavin (Mr. and Mrs. in real life) were the stars of *Airmail Mystery* (Universal 1932). *below:* Tom Tyler tries to pry the gun loose from the hand of LeRoy Mason in *Phantom of the Air* (Universal 1933). *bottom:* When two top stunt men go at it serial fans are really getting their money's worth. Yakima Canutt and Dave O'Brien went at it in *The Black Coin* (Weiss-Mintz 1936).

above: Harold "Red" Grange, one of the great football heroes of all time, played himself in the title role of *The Galloping Ghost* (Mascot 1931), his famous nickname. In this scene Grange is about to surprise veteran serial star-stunt man, Walter Miller. *left:* It was a youthful John Wayne who played the flying hero in *The Three Musketeers* (Mascot 1933). *below:* John Wayne has his hands full battling Al Ferguson, Charles King, and Glenn Strange in *Hurricane Express* (Mascot 1932).

A montage of favorite Republic serial heroes and villains drawn by noted artist Al Kilgore. The bell tower in the upper left-hand corner was Republic's trademark in the thirties and early forties before they switched to an eagle.

3. Republic Enters the Scene

WHEN REPUBLIC PICTURES CORPORATION started producing serials in 1936, few people expected anything of real merit to emerge from "that little studio out in the valley." Quite to everyone's surprise, after only a few short years they had perfected their screen action formats to a degree that was not to be matched by any other existing studio, major or minor. For Republic it was simply a matter of combining all the ingredients necessary to provide the best action recipe obtainable. Republic had unjustly earned the denigrating appellation of "Repulsive Pictures," and it was felt by most of Hollywood that working for "that" studio was the final step down the ladder to obscurity and unemployment. Like most underdogs, the Republic production staff refused to believe the charges leveled at them and, combining all their respective skills, they banded together to produce the finest product possible with the means available to them. That they succeeded so magnificently is a fitting tribute to all of them.

Much of the studio's serial success must be directly attributed to three superb action directors, William Witney, John English, and Spencer Gordon Bennet. Each of these men was able to portray on the screen action sequences of unparalleled excellence not readily envisioned in what appeared to be routine scripting. They instinctively knew how to "keep things moving,"

something Columbia and Universal were never able to do. Action and more action! That was what a serial needed, and that is what they contributed to it.

Witney and English co-directed seventeen consecutive masterpieces of serial entertainment that form what most of us nostalgically like to refer to as the golden age of serials. Starting in 1937 with *Zorro Rides Again*, the duo turned out, in succession, *The Lone Ranger, Fighting Devil Dogs, Dick Tracy Returns, Hawk of the Wilderness, The Lone Ranger Rides Again, Daredevils of the Red Circle, Dick Tracy's G-Men, Zorro's Fighting Legion, Drums of Fu Manchu, Adventures of Red Ryder, King of the Royal Mounted, Mysterious Dr. Satan, The Adventures of Captain Marvel, Jungle Girl, King of the Texas Rangers*, and finally, in 1941, *Dick Tracy vs. Crime, Inc.* Each serial, without exception, was crammed with action and visually excellent. The team split up in 1942, with English going into B-Western production at the studio, something Witney was similarly to do shortly thereafter. However, Witney was able on his own to continue to turn out exciting work like *Spy Smasher, Perils of Nyoka, King of the Mounties, G-Men vs. The Black Dragon*, and, after a three-year absence, *The Crimson Ghost*. English's only efforts during this period were *Daredevils of the West* in 1943, one of the most action-packed Western serials ever made, and, the following year, *Captain America*, the latter co-directed with Elmer Clifton.

With Spencer Gordon Bennet's arrival on the serial set came that great period of set destruction that is so closely identified with Republic films. While earlier fight choreography was inventive, it never equalled the heights obtained by Bennet. Working closely with his team of ace stunt men, usually headed by Tom Steele, with Dale Van Sickel, Eddie Parker, Duke Green, Ken Terrell, and Fred Graham joining in, Bennet literally reduced huge, ornately decorated, and liberally prop-laden sets to rubble in fight after fight, chapter after chapter. As he fondly recalls, "the bills for balsa wood were enormous." His very first serial for the studio, *Secret Service in Darkest Africa*, made in 1943, has to contain more fight sequences than any other serial ever made. Almost every one of the film's fifteen episodes contains three slugfests. To a somewhat lesser degree, but not *that* much less, his other Republic efforts were also filled with excitement enough to raise the pulse of even the most reserved serial viewer: *The Masked Marvel, The Tiger Woman, Haunted Harbor, Zorro's Black Whip, Manhunt of Mystery Island, Federal Operator 99, The Purple Monster Strikes, The Phantom Rider, King of the Forest Rangers, Daughter of Don Q, Son of Zorro,* and lastly, in 1947, *The Black Widow*. Although he received solo credit on only the first two serials (the remainder had Wallace Grissel, Yakima Canutt, and Fred Brannon alternately sharing the billing), all thirteen serials bore his unique stamp of quality. Bennet then joined Columbia Pictures, and one has only to view one of his epics there to determine how valuable Republic production was in creating top-notch screen fare.

A later chapter in this book will deal in detail with the superb stunt men who formed the Republic action team so necessary in creating the thousands of thrills which appear in the studio's sixty-six serial productions. Of major importance also was the studio's special-effects department, headed by Howard Lydecker, later assisted by his brother, Theodore. The hundreds of exploding cars, buildings, barns, planes, dams, and what-have-you turned out by this outstanding production unit were an integral factor in giving Republic its distinctive superiority in the serial field. Unlike Universal and Columbia with their cheaply done table-top miniatures, the Lydeck-ers used large-scale, meticulously detailed models and photographed them outside against natural skies. They were so lifelike that most of us really believed they were the actual full-size items. One has only to view the end of chapter one of *King of the Texas Rangers*, in which an entire miniature oil field goes up in flame, with huge, billowing balls of fire rising within the derrick frames, or the end of chapter one of *The Masked Marvel*, in which a blazing miniature truck blows up igniting a gas-filled model of a gigantic fuel storage tank, which in turn blows up, to realize the quality of work the Lydeckers turned out.

To single out one factor as being more important than any other is, under most circumstances, unfair when so many elements combine successfully to form a superior product. True, the fights, direction, and special effects *were* important, but so was the set decoration, editing, lighting, and photography, the latter accomplished primarily by William Nobles, Reggie Lanning and Bud Thackery during the golden age. And important also, to a greater degree than most people would realize, was the music. Republic was the only studio to utilize elaborately written original scores. William Lava's superb compositions for *Zorro's Fighting Legion, Dick Tracy's G-Men,* and *Daredevils of the Red Circle,* among others, are outstanding examples of film music that can strengthen the intrinsic values of the material it accompanies. Mort Glickman took over the music reins when Lava left to work at RKO and Warner Brothers, and quickly earned the title "King of the Chase Writers" with his superb scores for *Mysterious Dr. Satan, Spy Smasher, The Masked Marvel, Captain America,* and others. The music of both men was so good that Republic re-used the scores numerous times in subsequent serials, B-films, and Westerns. Lava referred recently to the writing of those early scores as turning out "music by the yard." It is an apt phrase, for the men were paid surprisingly little money for their work and ground it out at an amazing pace, often writing pieces while the recording sessions were in progress. It is a tribute to both men that, under these trying conditions, both were able to turn out such consistently outstanding material.

When the quality of Republic serials declined in the years after World War II, it was for economic reasons rather than professional deterioration of the producing staff. Herbert Yates knew the market for serials was declining, and he decided to spend as little as possible on their production, so that at the end, with *King of the Carnival* in 1955, there was hardly any comparison between the final efforts of the company and the greatness of the studio's serials of the thirties and early forties. It was a sad sight to witness.

Yet Republic's track record for success over the twenty-year period was meritorious enough to forget the few failures. From *Darkest Africa* in 1936 through sixty-five subsequent serial productions one can be enormously thankful for countless, and unforgettable, days of thrills and adventure.

A winged Bat Man attacks Clyde Beatty in the premier Republic serial, *Darkest Africa* (Republic 1936). Even in their first serial effort, some of the wonderful Howard Lydecker effects were brilliantly used and served as a generous preview of the greatness that was to emerge from the studio.

above: The Painted Stallion (Republic 1937) was a typical example of Republic's excellence in outdoor action films. The cast included (*left to right*) Ray Corrigan, Hoot Gibson (in a much smaller role than he deserved), Sammy McKim and Hal Taliaferro. *below:* Ray Mala, *left,* was of limited help to Herman Brix (later Bruce Bennett), who portrayed Kioga in the highly successful *Hawk of the Wilderness* (Republic 1938). Adding to the film's excitement was an exciting musical score by William Lava. *opposite page:* Ralph Byrd, in his only non-Dick Tracy role at Republic, is about to take a dangerous plunge with the assistance of Richard Alexander in *S.O.S. Coast Guard* (Republic 1937).

above: Herman Brix and Lee Powell were the *Fighting Devil Dogs* (Republic 1938) who battled one of the most famous of all serial villains, the Lightning. Although many regard it as a favorite, much of the serial is done in a rather routine fashion, but the music and special effects help to counteract the excessive use of stock footage. It certainly has to rank as one of the top-ten serials of all time. *below:* Another of Republic's all-time serial hits was *Daredevils of the Red Circle* (Republic 1939). The three leads were perfectly cast as circus performers who were on the trail of the escaped convict 39013 (Charles Middleton) as he attempted to sabotage various properties of the man he held responsible for his being sent to prison. The ending of chapter one is one of the greatest serial thrills yet seen on the screen, with Charles Quigley fleeing through a rapidly flooding tunnel on a motorcycle. In the scene below, David Sharpe, Herman Brix, and Charles Quigley find a clue which leads them to a daredevil climax at an oil refinery.

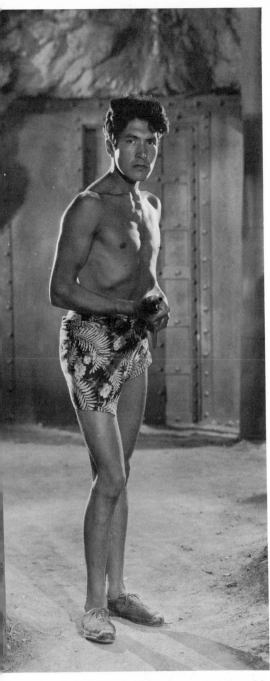

above: With daredevil stunt ace David Sharpe doing the action scenes for Robert Wilcox (as the Copperhead), *Mysterious Dr. Satan* (Republic 1940) was a serial-goer's delight. In this scene the Copperhead releases Ella Neal with the aid of William Newell from a death trap set by Dr. Satan (Eduardo Ciannelli).

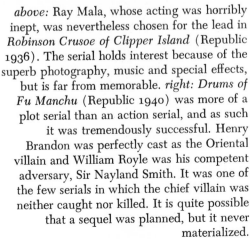

above: Ray Mala, whose acting was horribly inept, was nevertheless chosen for the lead in *Robinson Crusoe of Clipper Island* (Republic 1936). The serial holds interest because of the superb photography, music and special effects, but is far from memorable. *right: Drums of Fu Manchu* (Republic 1940) was more of a plot serial than an action serial, and as such it was tremendously successful. Henry Brandon was perfectly cast as the Oriental villain and William Royle was his competent adversary, Sir Nayland Smith. It was one of the few serials in which the chief villain was neither caught nor killed. It is quite possible that a sequel was planned, but it never materialized.

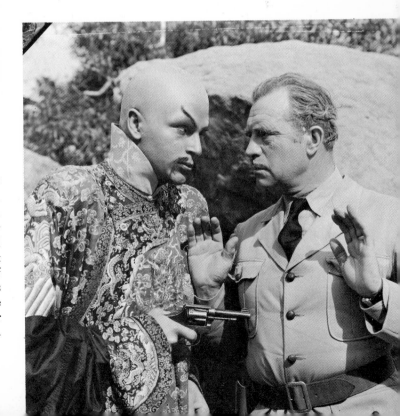

Tom Tyler was a perfect choice to portray the superhuman cartoon favorite in *The Adventures of Captain Marvel* (Republic 1941).

4. Comic Strips on the Screen

THE TREMENDOUS GROWTH in popularity of the newspaper adventure comic strip in the mid-thirties was bound to inspire the serial-producing film companies to bring America's new fictional heroes to the screen. Universal Pictures began the cycle with the popular airplane daredevil Tailspin Tommy, in two thrilling sky adventures in 1934's *Tailspin Tommy* and 1935's *Tailspin Tommy in the Great Air Mystery*. Using visually exciting stock shots from earlier Universal flying epics plus thrilling new footage, serial fans were delighted to see a favorite pencil-and-ink hero brought to vivid life. In 1936 Universal entered into an arrangement with King Features and obtained motion picture rights to an impressive list of Sunday newspaper favorites. Heading the list was Flash Gordon, who was brought to life by Buster Crabbe in three outstanding attractions, *Flash Gordon* (1936), *Flash Gordon's Trip to Mars* (1938), and *Flash Gordon Conquers the Universe* (1940). Viewed today, the three serials seem routine, rather cheaply produced and poorly acted, but to audiences who saw them in their original releases they were pure imaginative delight. Other popular action heroes brought "to life" by Universal included: *Ace Drummond*, another popular flying strip originally created by Captain Eddie Rickenbacker and starring John

King; *Jungle Jim*, with Grant Withers portraying Alex Raymond's creation; *Radio Patrol*, again with Withers playing the lead, this time as Pat O'Hara as he tried to solve a mystery surrounding an invention of "flexible steel"; *Tim Tyler's Luck*, with young Frankie Thomas chasing through the jungle in search of the elephants' graveyard, and being thwarted by the notorious Spider Webb; *Red Barry*, starring Buster Crabbe, on temporary leave from the planet Mongo, playing a detective investigating a Chinatown mystery; *Buck Rogers*, also with Crabbe in the title role, but decidedly cheaper in production values and excitement; *Don Winslow of the Navy* and *Don Winslow of the Coast Guard*, two wartime entries, both inexpensively mounted and using excessive quantities of newsreel stock footage. Don Terry as Winslow was an effective hero, however. Universal also brought Alex Raymond's agent-hero to the screen in two versions: the 1937 *Secret Agent X-9* had Scott Kolk battling conventional villains, while the 1945 *Secret Agent X-9*, portrayed by Lloyd Bridges, opposed the wartime Nazi menace. One of Universal's better film adaptations was the picturization of Zack Mosley's popular flying hero in *The Adventures of Smilin' Jack*, with young Tom Brown giving an excellent performance. In all, Universal adapted sixteen comic-strip heroes for screen serial treatment.

Running a close second, with fifteen adaptations, was Columbia Pictures. They began in 1939 with Warren Hull's imaginative portrayal of the famous King Features' top-hatted hero, *Mandrake the Magician*. The following year a most unsatisfactory version of *Terry and the Pirates* was made by the studio with William Tracy playing Terry and Granville Owens playing Pat Ryan. Directed by James Horne, as were so many of these early Columbia efforts, the result was childish and ineffective. Horne was tremendous at directing two-reel comedies, but he was completely out of his element in bringing thrills to the serial devotee. *The Batman* made his first appearance on the screen in 1943, portrayed by Lewis Wilson in the most ill-fitting costume one could imagine. Douglas Croft as Robin was equally unappealing. That same year, however, Tom Tyler brought a visual acceptance of his characterization of *The Phantom*. And the ladies finally got a chance to see one of their own get screen-time when *Brenda Starr, Reporter*, played by one of the darlings of the B-film crowd, Joan Woodbury, helped rid the big town of criminal elements. Ralph Byrd, trying once again to shed his Dick Tracy image, took to the saddle wearing a mask as *The Vigilante*, a popular character appearing in *Action Comics*. Kane Richmond, one of the more capable serial performers, tried to bring some kind of realism to the characterization of *Brick Bradford*, but the script defeated him, as it had defeated so many others at Columbia. When *Superman* finally made it to the serial screen in 1948, it was one of the few serials to play A theatres rather than the standard "scratch" houses. The showcasing really wasn't justified: Kirk Alyn was not effective in the title role, and the flying sequences, instead of being imaginably staged with miniatures, were simply cartoon dots jumping ludicrously around. The sequel two years later, *Atom Man vs. Superman*, was similarly ineffective. The remaining strips brought little distinction to the studio. *Tex Granger* was a weak Western starring Robert Kellard; *Congo Bill*, with Don McGuire, should have disappeared in one of its own quicksand bogs; *Bruce Gentry*, with Tom Neal, did have a little action, thanks to Tom Steele and Dale Van Sickel, who did the action work, but the serial provided more laughs than excitement; *Batman and Robin*, this time with Robert Lowery and Johnny Duncan in the roles of the Dynamic Duo, was a sorry sequel to the 1943 version; *Blackhawk* gave Kirk Alyn more to work with and wasn't half bad, and Buster Crabbe finished his serial career as the Mighty Thunda, who appeared to be considerably less than mighty in this stock-filled, back-lot jungle travesty based on the comic-strip hero, *King of the Congo*. In reviewing the total output, one would be hard put to consider more than three or four Columbia serials even adequate. However, the kids loved them all! They were fun, and, their poor quality notwithstanding, they brought the audiences back week after week to watch every one of them.

Republic only brought ten comic strips to life on the theatre screen, but their track record for success was almost one hundred percent. Dick Tracy was active in four separate thrill-packed adventures. *Dick Tracy*, the first of the four, was the slowest-moving of the group but was fascinating because of the superb mystery man, the Spider. *Dick Tracy Returns*, *Dick Tracy's G-Men*, and *Dick Tracy vs. Crime, Inc.* were all creative masterpieces, filled with location photography and imaginative action sequences. *Adventures of Red Ryder* brought screen stardom to its lead, Don "Red" Barry. Barry recently admitted that he hated doing the role because he felt that his physical appearance was not adequate to portray the tall, lanky red-haired cowboy on the screen. He was grateful, however, for the success it brought him, and the film was extremely successful. *King of the Royal Mounted* and *King of the Mounties* were both based on a character created by Zane Grey, which later found a large following on the comic pages across the country. Allan Lane was a perfect choice to play the leading role in both films, and Republic know-how made both films action-packed hits. Republic had tried to acquire screen rights to Superman but, when the copyright holders demanded too much control over the script, settled on the Fawcett Publications hero, Captain Marvel, in *The Adventures of Captain Marvel*. With Tom Tyler in the leading role, and David Sharpe providing all the stunt thrills, this serial was second only to Universal's *Flash Gordon* in popularity. Fawcett also gave Republic *Spy Smasher*, its second most popular character, and Kane Richmond brought more than an average amount of talent to the screen characterization of the spy-chasing hero. *Captain America* was Republic's final entry in the comic-strip sweepstakes, and it was superb in all aspects of production. Dick Purcell was ideal in the role and would have been an excellent choice to star in subsequent roles had he not died shortly after completing this film.

All three studios took liberties in the scripting of their films based on comic strips. The first *Flash Gordon* serial was the only one to even remotely follow the actual scripts used in the newspaper adventures. *Captain America* lost his regular partner Bucky, *Spy Smasher* suddenly acquired a twin brother, and *Dick Tracy* lost Pat Patton, Junior, and Tess Trueheart as that series progressed. But no one really cared. Each serial was judged on its own merits, and even though some had *no* merit, they were enjoyable film fare.

above: Continuing in the comic-strip vein, Tom Tyler also gave a strikingly acceptable image as *The Phantom* (Columbia 1943). *left:* Don McGuire, who went on to become a television director, was *Congo Bill* (Columbia 1948).

29

above: Grant Withers barely escapes being crushed to death in an elaborate trap in his role as Pat O'Hara of the *Radio Patrol* (Universal 1937). *right:* Captain America (Republic 1944) found Dick Purcell leaving behind his shield and companion, Bucky, as he battled the evil Scarab. *below:* Al Ferguson (*left*) and Charles "Slim" Whitaker get the drop on Maurice Murphy as *Tailspin Tommy* (Universal 1934) and Grant Withers.

Donald Barry became "Red" Barry after he starred in *Adventures of Red Ryder*
(Republic 1940).

Frankie Thomas as Tim and Frances Robinson try to escape from someone, or something, in *Tim Tyler's Luck* (Universal 1937).

left: John King was *Ace Drummond* (Universal 1936), a flying ace created for the newspaper strip by Captain Eddie Rickenbacker. *below, left:* Kane Richmond played a dual role in *Spy Smasher* (Republic 1942). Frank Corsaro was his Free French assistant. *below, right: Mandrake the Magician* (Columbia 1939), based on the popular King Features strip, had Warren Hull in the title role matching wits with the mysterious Wasp.

above: Irving Pichel and Walter Miller
(*far left and right*) apparently have
Ralph Byrd as Dick Tracy and his partner,
Ted Pearson, finally trapped in *Dick Tracy's
G-Men* (Republic 1939). *left:* Tom Brown
had to contend with many perils like this
in *Adventures of Smilin' Jack* (Universal
1943).

Kirk Alyn rescues Noel Neill as Lois Lane with a minor show of strength in
Superman (Columbia 1948).

above: Scott Kolk was Alex Raymond's famous *Secret Agent X-9* (Universal 1937), ably assisted by the lovely Jean Rogers. *right:* Buster Crabbe, among other comic favorites, was also *Red Barry* (Universal 1938). *below:* Buster Crabbe as Flash protects Jean Rogers from the evil spells cast by Beatrice Roberts in *Flash Gordon's Trip to Mars* (Universal 1938).

above: Robert Lowery as the Caped Crusader and John Duncan as Robin point out some facts to Lyle Talbot in *Batman and Robin* (Columbia 1949). *below:* Granville Owens as Pat Ryan lends a helping hand to William Tracy as Terry Lee in *Terry and the Pirates* (Columbia 1940).

This is how Zorro made his first serial entrance in chapter one of *Zorro Rides Again* (Republic 1937). John Carroll played the popular masked hero of early California.

5. The Descendants of Zorro

OF ALL THE MASKED HEROES who graced the serial screen, none was more durable than that masked avenger of the Old West, Zorro. The character was originally created by Johnston McCulley for his story, *The Curse of Capistrano*, which appeared in installments in 1919 in the pulp magazine *All-Story*. The story was a simple tale of a masked man who went about early California avenging the wrongs committed upon the peons by an unscrupulous governor. The hero's identity was not revealed until the conclusion, but Don Diego Vega was the only logical choice from nearly the beginning.

The story was first brought to the screen in 1920 as *The Mark of Zorro*, starring the athletic Douglas Fairbanks, Sr., and was full of action and thrills in the well-known Fairbanks tradition. In 1925 *Don Q, Son of Zorro* had Fairbanks playing Cesar de Vega, the son of the original Zorro. Although in essence a sequel, it was not based on McCulley's work, but on a story written by K. and Hesketh Prichard called *Don Q's Love Story* and adapted by scriptwriters Jack Cunningham and Lotta Woods. In 1937 Republic brought the character to the screen for the first time in a sound film called *The Bold Caballero*, starring the likable Robert Livingston as an "original" masked Zorro in the studio's first film photographed in "Natural Color."

Finally, in 1937 Republic decided to feature the famous character in one of their serial adventures. They chose a relative newcomer named John Carroll to play the role of James Vega, who was the great-grandson of the original Don Diego Vega. He was excellent in the role, with the possible exception of the few times he was required to burst into song. A singing "masked avenger" was too much! The exciting story found villains Noah Beery, Sr., and Richard Alexander out to destroy the California–Yucatan Railroad. Particularly effective were scenes actually photographed at a dam site and other superior outdoor locations. Handling the stunt chores for Carroll was veteran daredevil Yakima Canutt, who provided many thrills and handled the bullwhip in superlative fashion. Released under the title *Zorro Rides Again*, the serial was also edited into a feature version under the same title, and was re-released in the late fifties to cash in on the interest in the character generated by Walt Disney with his television series.

As fine as *Zorro Rides Again* was, *Zorro's Fighting Legion*, released two years later, was even better. Reed Hadley (whose voice was so outstanding that Twentieth Century-Fox was later to use him as the narrator for such quality films as *Guadalcanal Diary* and *The House on 92nd Street*) was in superior form portraying alternately the foppish Diego and Zorro, the dashing masked rider who appeared whenever danger threatened. One of the primary reasons for the serial's success was the incorporation into the screenplay of one of the better mystery villains, Don Del Oro. This reincarnation of a Yaqui god was, in reality, one of the four members of a Council. Contrary to good ethical conduct, this metal-helmeted devil was inciting the Indians to revolt, and it took all his courage, as well as twelve full episodes, for Zorro to unmask the villain, who was ultimately destroyed in a fiery pit by the very Indians he had duped. Contributing to the overall effect of the film was a magnificent score largely composed by William Lava.

Five years went by before Zorro was again to appear, or rather *seem* to appear, in another Republic serial. In *Zorro's Black Whip* there was never any mention of Zorro in the entire serial. Linda Stirling played a character called the Whip and certainly dressed in an outfit resembling the famed avenger's, but no direct tie-up was ever made. Perhaps the writers felt that the name should never be used for the female of the species. Johnston McCulley was given a credit line stating that he created the Zorro character, but that was all there was to it. The story itself was a rather routine Western tale with scheming Francis MacDonald out to control the entire territory and being thwarted at every turn by luscious Linda and George J. Lewis, the latter seen in a welcome change of pace from his usual villainous roles.

In *Son of Zorro*, made in 1947, the mystery man, called the Chief, was out to grab some territory for himself and misused various public offices to further his schemes. Riding to the aid of the town after returning from the Civil War was George Turner (a likable performer whose career was surprisingly brief). Recalling that one of his ancestors had dressed as Zorro many years before to right wrongs, he decides to bring the masked man back once again to help solve the current situation. Peggy Stewart was the damsel in distress, and the mystery man turned out to be—well, either Edmund Cobb, Ken Terrell, Tom London or Edward Cassidy.

The final entry in the Zorro series was *Ghost of Zorro*, released in 1949. Chosen for the lead this time was Clayton Moore, who was just beginning his long-running role as television's Lone Ranger. Moore was a popular leading man at Republic and was particularly effective in Westerns. As Zorro, he cut a striking figure in the saddle in this tale of a community trying to build a telegraph line and being besieged by Eugene Roth's savage henchmen, including Roy Barcroft. A fair amount of stock footage from earlier Zorro films was used and, in chapter one, a complete sequence was used from the studio's 1943 success, *Daredevils of the West*. For some strange reason, they dubbed in a "mystery voice" for Moore, something they had not bothered to do in any of the other films in the series. At the same time *Zorro Rides Again* was released in feature form in the fifties, *Ghost of Zorro* was also edited and released as a companion film to fill neighborhood theatre double bills.

Although the series had been officially concluded with *Ghost of Zorro*, Republic did release two serials which utilized a masked hero who looked exactly like Zorro, and contained a considerable amount of stock footage from the earlier Zorro serials. *Don Daredevil Rides Again* in 1951 had Ken Curtis, now of television's *Gunsmoke* fame, playing a routine Western hero wearing a Zorro costume in order to match old and new footage. The same was done by Richard Simmons in 1954's *Man with the Steel Whip*. It was a sad finish for the dashing avenger.

Through the years there were a great many pseudo-Zorros who rode the Western range dealing out swift justice. Robert Livingston may have been called the Eagle in *The Vigilantes Are Coming*, but he certainly looked like Zorro. And the Lone Ranger might very easily be termed an Americanized version of the avenging rider.

When Disney brought Zorro to the home audience he reduced the action elements and increased the comedy. He did give the character a more dashing costume, with a silken black cape flowing in the breeze as Zorro rode through the night. None of the Republic Zorros had worn a cloak. One of the strange coincidences that occasionally occur in film-making happened when William Lava, who almost twenty years before had written the background music for *Zorro's Fighting Legion,* was signed to compose the music for the new television series. Alas, if only they could have gotten Reed Hadley to play the role of Zorro in the series instead of Guy Williams.

All in all, though, the masked avenger did all right for himself on the screen.

Don Del Oro, the mysterious masked villain, orders the death of Paul Marian
and Zorro (Reed Hadley) in *Zorro's Fighting Legion* (Republic 1939). Holding
the gun on Zorro in the center of the picture is Jim Pierce, one of the many
stars who played Tarzan on the screen.

above: Zorro's primary opponent in *Zorro Rides Again* (Republic 1937) was veteran badman Richard Alexander. That's John Carroll under the mask. *left:* Reed Hadley's was most likely the best of all the serial Zorro characterizations. His voice, used frequently for narration in Twentieth Century-Fox semidocumentary films, lent the proper authority to the masked hero and was subtly used to portray the foppish alter ego, Diego Vegas. *Zorro's Fighting Legion* (Republic 1939) also had a superb musical score by William Lava to add to the film's overall success.

6. Science Fiction

IN THE PRESENT WORLD where atomic bombs and men traveling to the moon are commonplace, it is hard to imagine that young viewers only thirty-five years ago were going into ecstasy over some toy rocketships and balloon-like artificial planets portrayed on a motion picture screen. However, such was the case when Universal presented Buster Crabbe in 1936 as *Flash Gordon*. Here truly was adventure on a grand scale, previously pictured only on the Sunday comic pages or in the novels of such creative writers as Jules Verne. Here were no ordinary G-men cracking down on racketeers or marshals rounding up outlaws; instead, there was Ming the Merciless, a dweller of the planet Mongo, out to destroy the world, and only one man, Flash Gordon, capable of battling the scheming devil. And it wasn't just Ming poor Flash had to worry about. Along the way there were Shark Men, Hawk Men, Orangapoids, Octosacs, and other assorted monstrosities to deal with, and deal with them he did, to everyone's satisfaction. *Flash Gordon* was so popular that Universal brought Crabbe back to play Alex Raymond's fantastic hero in two subsequent serials, *Flash Gordon's Trip to Mars* and *Flash Gordon Conquers the Universe*, each time battling Ming, who seemed to be indestructible. It was fun in the grand style.

A year earlier, Mascot had introduced Gene Autry to stardom in *The Phantom Empire*. Gene played a singing cowboy who suddenly found himself journeying, via a secret cave entrance, to the futuristic city of Murania far below the surface of the earth, where he met the beautiful queen Tika (Dorothy Christy), who was bent on world domination. Murania was peopled with the mysterious Thunder Riders, who frequently ventured aboveground, much to the consternation of Gene, Frankie Darro, and Betsy King Ross. Adding to the confusion were robots (used again many years later in the Columbia serial, *Captain Video*) and assorted death-dealing devices. The exciting finale had a wildly gyrating ray-gun destroying the entire underground city accompanied by the rousing strains of "Storm and War," a thrilling piece of music often used in Westerns and serials of the thirties. The "destruction" of the city was accomplished by printing a photo of it on a film with thick emulsion, then photographing it in slow motion while the print was heated; the heat of course caused the emulsion to run. This same effect was used in several later Republic serials whenever a mountain had to melt, as in *The Adventures of Captain Marvel*, *S.O.S. Coast Guard*, and *King of the Rocket Men*.

Republic, obviously trying to cash in on the

enormous success expected from Universal's release of *Flash Gordon,* came out with their own science-fiction adventure, *Undersea Kingdom,* the very same year. With the advanced special effects of Howard Lydecker, the undersea city of Atlantis had much more eye-appeal than Murania or Mongo. The story found Ray "Crash" Corrigan playing a naval officer who is sent in a newly developed submarine to discover the underwater cause of a series of devastating earthquakes terrorizing the world. The mystery is solved, after twelve action-packed chapters, and the underground city destroyed. One chapter ending found Crash tied to the front of an armored vehicle which Lon Chaney, Jr., intended to plunge into the heavy gates of an enemy fort. When threatened with death unless he cooperated, Crash heroically shouted, "Go ahead and *ram!*" Now *that* was really a *hero!*

With Buster Crabbe's outstanding success as Flash Gordon, it was only natural that Universal would cast the handsome leading man as Buck Rogers in 1939. By all standards of previous production, this serial should really have been a quality product. However, it turned out to be a rather routine effort, with Buck battling his traditional newspaper foe, Killer Kane (Anthony Warde), who spent most of his time converting humans into robots via a powerful helmet he had developed. Henry Brandon, who was to portray Fu Manchu a year later, was excellent as Kane's chief henchman, and David Sharpe could be seen playing roles on both Kane's side and Buck's team, as well as doubling for young Jackie Moran.

Brick Bradford, with Kane Richmond as the comic-strip hero, started out in its early episodes with several interesting gimmicks including a "crystal door" which, when passed through, could transport one molecularly to the moon, and a "time top" which could send its occupants back in time to earlier centuries. The ideas were inventive enough to hook audiences for the first half of the serial, but after those early thrills the remainder of the serial turned into a straight everyday action drama. This was a rather poor showing from Columbia in 1947, but *Superman* was on the way.

The Purple Monster Strikes was an action-packed Republic serial of 1945 with a most interesting plot. The Purple Monster arrives on Earth from the planet Mars in a small spaceship which is consumed in flames shortly after he leaves it. He locates Dr. Cyrus Layton, a renowned scientist, and informs him that he has been sent to Earth in order to learn how to build a much more sophisticated spacecraft. When Layton refuses to cooperate, the Monster takes a small vial of Martian gas and kills the scientist. With this same gas the Monster is able to "enter" the body of the dead man and assume his personality. The remainder of the serial is strictly action and more action as the Monster seeks all the necessary supplies needed to build the spaceship. Roy Barcroft was superb as the Monster and Dennis Moore and Linda Stirling played effectively as the protagonists.

Radar Men from the Moon, made seven years later, found Barcroft in his same Purple Monster costume, but now portraying Retik, a leader of Moonmen intent on conquering the world. Obviously he had been taking lessons from Ming the Merciless. The serial utilized quite a bit of footage from *The Purple Monster Strikes,* including the entire finale, which depicted the aliens' spaceship being blasted from the skies.

Flying Disc Man from Mars and *Zombies of the Stratosphere,* two serials released by Republic in the fifties, also dealt with aliens from other planets landing on Earth. In the former, the Disc Man was seeking aid in building atomic-powered planes and bombs to take over Earth and make it a satellite of Mars; the latter found the Zombies trying to build a hydrogen device capable of blowing the Earth out of its orbit, thus allowing them to let their planet "inherit" the orbit to take advantage of our superior atmosphere. Worthy ambitions, but completely thwarted by the noble heroes.

And how about all those lost civilizations, active and inactive, sought after in serials like *Terry and the Pirates, Darkest Africa, The Lost City,* and *Call of the Savage?* They deserve mention, as do all those serials which utilized mad inventions to further their inventor's wildest dreams: serials like *The Phantom Creeps, Mysterious Dr. Satan, The Vanishing Shadow,* and *The Monster and the Ape,* which had incredible robots doing their master's bidding; and *The Crimson Ghost* with his "cyclotrode," Dr. Vulcan in *King of the Rocket Men* with his "decimator," and so many others. They made it very plain that, perhaps, Earth wasn't so bad after all if our heroes were able to successfully challenge so many attempts to conquer and destroy civilization.

left: Buster Crabbe as Flash Gordon rescues
Carol Hughes from one of the perils on Frigia
in *Flash Gordon Conquers the Universe*
(Universal 1940). *below:* Kane Richmond
and Claudia Dell discovered the mysterious
city in the jungle in *The Lost City* (Krellberg,
1935). That's Joseph Swickard, Eddie Fether-
stone, and Sam Baker in the background.

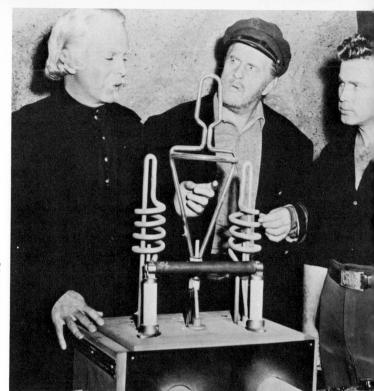

right: Jules Verne's *Mysterious Island* (Columbia 1951) came to the screen in serial form with Leonard Penn, Eugene Roth, and, in the lead, Richard Crane. *below:* The robot from *Mysterious Dr. Satan* (Republic 1940) made a return appearance in *Zombies of the Stratosphere* (Republic 1952). That's Judd Holdren (or his stunt double) under the helmet.

left: Captain Video was a popular television hero in the early fifties. He was portrayed by, among others, Al Hodge, who had played the Green Hornet on radio. When *Captain Video* (Columbia 1951) was transferred to the screen, Judd Holdren played the title role. *below:* Judd Holdren seemed to have a monopoly on playing science-fiction heroes in the early fifties. In this scene from *The Lost Planet* (Columbia 1953), Holdren, *right,* gets some scientific information from veteran character actor Forrest Taylor.

In *The Phantom Empire* (Mascot 1935) singing cowboy Gene Autry discovered
the underground city of Murania. In this scene he gets the drop on Stanley
Blystone.

left: Gregory Gay in an absurd publicity shot for *Flying Disc Man from Mars* (Republic 1951).
below: C. Montague Shaw and Lon Chaney, Jr., seem to have Ray "Crash" Corrigan at a disadvantage in the *Undersea Kingdom* (Republic 1936).

above: Roy Barcroft as the mysterious alien from Mars is about to inhabit the body of James Craven in the exciting serial *The Purple Monster Strikes* (Republic 1945). *right:* The pursuers they've spotted will not prevent Kane Richmond and Linda Johnson from taking a ride in the "time top" in the serial version of the popular King Features' comic strip *Brick Bradford* (Columbia 1947).

left: Millburn Stone demonstrates one of the mysterious devices uncovered in *The Great Alaskan Mystery* (Universal 1944). *below:* George Wallace is under the mask in *Radar Men from the Moon* (Republic 1952).

above: Bela Lugosi demonstrates one of his inventions to henchman Jack C. Smith in *The Phantom Creeps* (Universal 1939). *right:* Tristram Coffin was the unlikely hero in *King of the Rocket Men* (Republic 1949). This was Republic's last really noteworthy serial, and stock from this film was used in three subsequent serial adventures: *Flying Disc Man from Mars* (Republic 1951), *Radar Men from the Moon* (Republic 1952), and *Zombies of the Stratosphere* (Republic 1952).

Tom Mix, in his last starring film, takes care of Tom London in *The Miracle Rider* (Mascot 1935).

7. Hit the Saddle

ALMOST WITHOUT EXCEPTION, the production schedule of each studio's annual serial output would include at least one Western serial. The primary reasons for this were economy and popularity. Westerns were relatively inexpensive to produce: few costly and involved interior sets had to be built, and exteriors could be easily photographed on appropriate sites within a few miles of the studio, if indeed not right on the producing company's back lot. And, of course, Westerns were popular, tremendously popular, during those Saturday-afternoon adventure orgies. Cowboy stars like Buck Jones, Ken Maynard, Tim McCoy, and Tom Tyler were money in the bank to the companies, and so it was to their advantage to have them appear in serials that would bring their fans back for twelve or fifteen consecutive weeks to follow their adventures.

Of all the heroes who hit the saddle on behalf of justice, none was more popular than Buck Jones. A no-nonsense performer who was a capable actor and an excellent rider, Buck gave robust performances in *Gordon of Ghost City, The Red Rider, The Roaring West, The Phantom Rider, White Eagle,* and *Riders of Death Valley.* Many more titles might have been added to the list if Buck had not died so tragically in the Coconut Grove fire in 1942, in which he

became a real-life hero by rescuing trapped patrons time after time until he was overcome by the smoke.

Johnny Mack Brown started his film career playing romantic leads. Fortunately, he very quickly found his niche in films as one of the most popular of Western performers on the screen. Beginning with Mascot's 1933 production of *Fighting with Kit Carson,* Johnny moved to Universal and starred in four more action classics: *Rustlers of Red Dog, Wild West Days, Flaming Frontiers,* and *Oregon Trail.* In the case of both Jones and Johnny Mack Brown, the earlier serials were well photographed and inventively done, and the later ones showed obvious signs of cheapness, including many stock shots from the previous efforts.

Tom Tyler was one of the few cowboy stars who was able to leave his horse behind from time to time in order to play non-Western heroes. Although he is thought of primarily as a Western star, only two of his seven starring serials were Westerns: *Phantom of the West,* made by Mascot in 1931, and *Battling with Buffalo Bill,* a Universal release that same year. His popularity, due to B-Westerns, was such, however, that in 1932 and 1933 Universal starred him in three out of four consecutively produced chapter plays: *Jungle Mystery, Clancy of the*

59

Mounted, and *Phantom of the Air.* In the forties he had the distinction of playing two of the most famous comic-strip characters on the serial screen in *The Adventures of Captain Marvel* and *The Phantom.*

Tim McCoy, or, as many like to refer to him today, Colonel Tim, has the unique distinction of having been the star of the first all-talking serial, *The Indians Are Coming,* which also was released in an all-silent version to accommodate those theatres that had not yet converted to the new sound system. The serial had a great many thrills but also a considerable amount of stock, which seriously detracted from its effectiveness. Still, it was an outstanding success and played at major theatres all over the country. Tim only made one other serial, the non-Western *Heroes of the Flames* in 1931.

William Elliott, another popular Western star, got his start in films by playing "society" extra roles, usually wearing a tuxedo. When he did venture into Western production, he was usually the heavy rather than the hero. However, with Columbia's 1938 production of *The Great Adventures of Wild Bill Hickok,* Elliott was on his way to the "Western Hall of Fame" and had acquired his famous "Wild Bill" nickname. He starred in two other Western serials for Columbia, *Overland with Kit Carson* and *The Valley of Vanishing Men,* as well as a popular series of B-Westerns, before moving over to Republic where he became a top Western favorite but made no serials.

Several top-drawer Western stars made appearances in serials produced by Mascot Pictures in the early thirties, including an old pro, Tom Mix, and an upcoming troubadour named Gene Autry. For Tom Mix, *The Miracle Rider* was his final starring film as well as his only serial. As a Texas Ranger in the film, Tom was trying to prevent scheming white men from stealing Indian land containing rare mineral deposits which they wanted for use in a new explosive, X-94. The aging star was showing his years, and much of the serial was very routine.

Gene Autry fared a great deal better in *The Phantom Empire.* Here was an exciting serial tale that had Autry bouncing like a rubber ball above ground and below to the underground scientific city of Murania. It seems the poor radio cowboy had to make a singing appearance every day on his radio show or lose a valuable contract. The sets were imaginative and the performances above average, and Gene was

launched on the road to a successful Western career.

Ken Maynard also had his chance to ride his horse Tarzan into thrilling mystery adventure when he took twelve thrilling episodes to uncover the menacing Rattler and solve the riddle of *Mystery Mountain.* Ken, a very pleasant personality, was beginning to put on weight, and his earlier fame was beginning to wear a little thin. No future serials turned up for the once-outstanding range ace, although he continued to turn out some surprisingly good Western features.

Harry Carey, whom more people remember as a character actor than as a Western star, also received Mascot exploitation in vehicles like *The Devil Horse* and *The Vanishing Legion.*

And among the many other stars and personalities who made one or more forays into the Western field were: Lon Chaney, Jr., as a Zorro-type avenger in RKO's solo serial effort, *The Last Frontier,* and at Universal in *Overland Mail;* Dick Foran, another popular singing cowboy starring in Warner Brothers features, in *Winners of the West* and *Riders of Death Valley;* Clayton Moore, television's Lone Ranger and a popular serial star at Republic in *Jesse James Rides Again, Adventures of Frank and Jesse James, Ghost of Zorro,* and *Son of Geronimo;* Jock Mahoney, a superb stunt man and one of the many Tarzans, in *Roar of the Iron Horse, Cody of the Pony Express,* and *Gunfighters of the Northwest;* Don "Red" Barry, in the serial that made him a star and gave him his nickname of "Red," *Adventures of Red Ryder;* Ray Corrigan, one of Republic's famous "Three Mesquiteers," in *The Painted Stallion;* and all the leading men in the Lone Ranger and Zorro series of chapter plays. The list seems endless, but of all the Western serials, perhaps the most action-packed among them was the Republic thriller of 1943, *Daredevils of the West.* Starring Allan Lane and Kay Aldridge, this serial had all the ingredients necessary to provide a dozen exciting episodes. Directed by John English, the film had a thrilling Indian chase in chapter one (later re-used in a cut-down version in *Ghost of Zorro*), top-notch fight sequences, including a masterpiece in which heroine Aldridge apparently fell into a refining vat, and an excellent script which allowed the leads to move from thrill to thrill with little letup. Add to that combination an exciting Mort Glickman musical score and inventive Howard Lydecker miniatures, and you had to have a perfect serial.

right: Johnny Mack Brown, one of the most popular of all the Western serial stars, in *Wild West Days* (Universal 1937). *below:* Buck Jones comes to the aid of Madge Bellamy in *Gordon of Ghost City* (Universal 1933).

right: Johnny Mack Brown would like a little information from Edward Hearn in *Fighting with Kit Carson* (Mascot 1933). *below:* William Haade, taking a hint from Tom Mix in the scene below, tries to get away from Allan Lane in *Daredevils of the West* (Republic 1943).

above: Ken Maynard had able help from Syd Saylor and Verna Hillie in trying to track down the Rattler in *Mystery Mountain* (Mascot 1934). *top:* Duncan Renaldo was "Slingin' Sammy" Baugh's Mexican confederate in *King of the Texas Rangers* (Republic 1941). Baugh was a popular football star, but his acting left quite a bit to be desired.

Harry Carey, one of the most beloved of all Western heroes and character actors, played the lead in *The Vanishing Legion* (Mascot 1931). In this scene Bob Kortman, *right*, is about to get an unexpected surprise.

above: Buck Jones' next to last serial was *White Eagle* (Columbia 1941) with Dorothy Fay. *below:* William Elliott earned his "Wild Bill" nickname in *The Great Adventures of Wild Bill Hickok* (Columbia 1938); here he is with Frankie Darro and Chief Thundercloud.

above: Clayton Moore gets the drop on David Sharpe, stunt man extraordinaire, and George J. Lewis in *Adventures of Frank and Jesse James* (Republic 1948). Moore played Jesse, out to right his name by paying back some of the money he had stolen earlier. *right:* Dickie Moore, former child star, was young Bill Cody, assisted by Jock O'Mahoney in *Cody of the Pony Express* (Columbia 1950).

Dick Foran, *right,* one of the screen's first singing cowboys, argues a point with veteran badman Harry Woods in *Winners of the West* (Universal 1940).

Paul Guilfoyle was supposedly under the hood in *The Scarlet Horseman* (Universal 1946), one of Universal's last serials.

above: Very few serials had an Indian hero, but one of the better ones was *Black Arrow* (Columbia 1944), starring Robert Scott, *right,* and Chief Thundercloud. *below:* The "Million-Dollar Serial," so called because of the tremendous cast, was *Riders of Death Valley* (Universal 1941) and starred Buck Jones, Noah Berry, Jr., Dick Foran, Guinn "Big Boy" Williams and Leo Carrillo. Also featured were Charles Bickford and Lon Chaney, Jr.

Robert Livingston was the Eagle, a semi-Zorro character in *The Vigilantes Are Coming* (Republic 1936) assisted by Guinn "Big Boy" Williams.

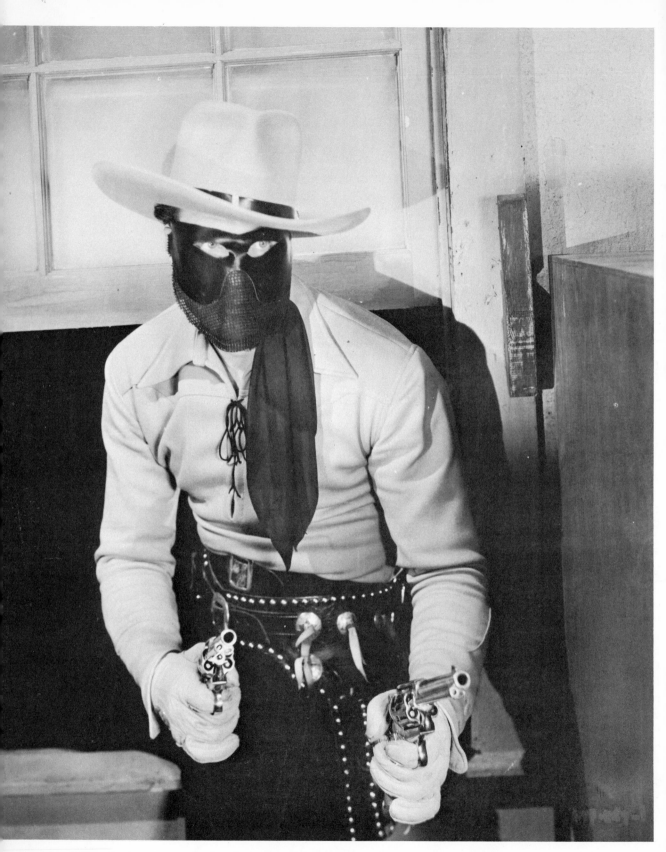

Robert Livingston was the "masked rider of the plains" in *The Lone Ranger Rides Again* (Republic 1939). This second, and final, serial based on the popular radio show was closer to the character than the first, also made by Republic, but it still lacked the "integrity" of the radio show's portrayal by allowing other cast members as well as the audience to know the Lone Ranger's real identity.

8. From Radio and the Pulps

I DON'T KNOW how many of you sat in front of your radios night after night during the forties with your latest "Captain Midnight Secret Decoder" clenched tightly in your hot little hands, waiting for the end of each adventure when announcer Pierre Andre would come on the air. Andre would give us listeners who formed the home "Secret Squadron" our latest message to decipher. What matter if the message turned out to be "Drink Ovaltine"—it was fun just to work the decoder. It was, therefore, with some relish that I looked forward to seeing one of my favorite heroes on the serial screen when Columbia announced they would release *Captain Midnight* in 1942. But even Dave O'Brien, playing the title role, could not save a script that was so juvenile it insulted the intelligence of children. One chapter ending had the hero trapped in a closet that was slowly filling with water, a reasonable enough peril to accept. But Columbia writers had to embellish the situation: they had a netlike device descend from the ceiling and push O'Brien's head down into the ascending water. The poor devil looked like a pretzel by the final fade-out.

Captain Midnight was only one of the many serials whose leading characters were derived from early pulp magazines and radio favorites. Of all the radio and pulp heroes, perhaps none was more famous than that slinking figure of the night who knew "what evil lurks in the hearts of men"—the Shadow. After nearly a decade of popularity in *Shadow Magazine* and on the airwaves, Columbia brought the character to the serial screen in 1940. Starring Victor Jory in the title role, the film was mediocre. The writers took many liberties with the character, including having Lamont Cranston frequently pose as a ridiculous-looking Oriental called Lin Chang. Audiences looked forward to seeing a man with the incredible ability to "cloud men's minds so they could not see him." Instead there was only a typical masked hero behaving rather like an imbecile. When Monogram Pictures made a brief series of features based on the character, the results were much more satisfactory.

In the early part of this century, Burt L. Standish's fictional hero Frank Merriwell was the idol of every red-blooded American boy. A college hero, Merriwell was an all-around champion athlete and adventurer. Universal brought this prototype of Jack Armstrong to the screen in 1936 in *The Adventures of Frank Merriwell*. Don Briggs played the lead, ably assisted by John King and pert Jean Rogers. Also in the cast were the sons of many favorite character actors of the time, including Wallace Reid, Jr., House Peters, Jr., Allan Hersholt, Edward Arnold, Jr., and Bryant Washburn, Jr. The plot had Frank involved in everything from winning sport contests to working in lumber camps and trying to prevent train crashes. It was what every boy in the audience dreamed *his* later years should be like.

Characters were often embellished in their translation to the screen. An excellent example of this appeared in the serial version of the popular Western radio show, *The Lone Ranger*. The origin of the character on radio was relatively simple: a band of Texas Rangers was ambushed and killed, with the exception of a sole survivor who was discovered and nursed back to health by the Indian Tonto. The survivor, taking the name of the Lone Ranger, avenged the deaths of his comrades and continued to fight for law and order for almost three decades on the radio. The Republic screenplay had the same basic origin, but a unique "mystery" angle was added. The audience was presented with five suspects, who were eliminated one by one until the Lone Ranger was unmasked in the last episode. It was an added bit of creative tampering that audiences did not find offensive.

The sequel, *The Lone Ranger Rides Again*, made a year later, in 1939, gave up the mystery angle altogether, and hero Robert Livingston was shown to be the masked man right from the first episode. Thus he was more like Zorro than radio's "masked rider of the plains."

The Green Hornet was another popular radio personality who was transferred to the screen in two action adventures. Gordon Jones first played the character in *The Green Hornet*, released by Universal in 1940. The routine script had the Hornet battling conventional racketeers. The popular success of the serial was such that Universal released a sequel, *The Green Hornet Strikes Again*, the very same year. This time Warren Hull played the role of the masked avenger. Playing Kato in both versions was Keye Luke.

Gang Busters was one of those serials that really had little to do with its namesake. On the radio, *Gang Busters* was a weekly show depicting various criminals receiving their ultimate just deserts from law enforcement officials. The screenplay for the 1942 Universal release was a typically serial-oriented thriller which had hero Kent Taylor battling the League of Murdered Men. Heading this criminal combine was Ralph Morgan, who ultimately met his end in a subway tunnel. The script was more reminiscent of something that might have been done on *The Shadow* or *The Green Hornet*.

Two more popular radio shows of the forties were brought to the screen by Columbia with only average success. John Hart appeared too old to play the "hero of Hudson High" in 1947's *Jack Armstrong,* although Pierre Watkin was ideal as Uncle Jim Fairfield. A little more acceptable to youthful audiences was William Bakewell as the flying ace, *Hop Harrigan,* released in 1946. Both serials reflected cheap production and weak scripts.

Almost as popular in the early pulps as the Shadow was the Spider, "Master of Men." Wearing a huge cape and mask, the Spider was one of the more colorful adventure heroes dealing out his own brand of justice to the underworld. Warren Hull, one of the more personable and talented serial leads, starred as the Spider in two Columbia productions, *The Spider's Web* in 1938 and *The Spider Returns* in 1941. Both serials had the benefit of mystery men, the Octopus in the first and the Gargoyle in the second. To show how ineffectual director James V. Horne was, in one scene of *The Spider Returns* he actually had two of the villain's henchmen playing "patty-cake" in the background. Knox Manning, a popular newscaster, was the narrator whose voice was heard at the end of each chapter of Columbia serials as previews of next week's episode were shown. Over a scene of two of the Gargoyle's henchmen boarding a train to commit mayhem, Manning was required to ask, "Why are these men boarding the train? Do they have their *tickets?*"

Perhaps the Shadow, the Green Hornet, the Spider, Jack Armstrong, the Lone Ranger, and all the others should have stayed where the imagination could conjure up its own mental portraits of them. They really didn't receive fair treatment on the screen.

adio's *Hop Harrigan* (Columbia 1946) was brought to the screen with William Bakewell in the title role. In this scene, Hop (*second from right*) is assisted by Sumner Getchell ("Tank Tinker"), obert "Buzz" Henry, and Jennifer Holt.

Warren Hull was the Green Hornet and Keye Luke was Kato in *The Green Hornet Strikes Again* (Universal 1940). Gas gun and all, this second serial version suffered in comparison with the first because of the amount of stock footage used. Warren Hull was superior, however, to Gordon Jones in the title role.

Of all the pulp heroes perhaps none was more famous than Burt L. Standish's Frank Merriwell. Don Briggs was an excellent choice to play the young hero in *The Adventures of Frank Merriwell* (Universal 1936).

above: Gordon Jones brought radio's famous Green Hornet to the screen in 1940. The film remained generally faithful to the character presented on the air. *The Green Hornet* (Universal 1940) has not been reissued since its original presentation, even to capitalize on the fame of the television series done in 1967 at the height of the "camp" craze. *below:* Dave O'Brien was a popular actor-stunt man and brought a degree of professionalism to the title role of *Captain Midnight* (Columbia 1942) based on the popular radio serial. However, the writing was ludicrous, and the serial was far from satisfying.

above: In the first serial version of the radio show *The Lone Ranger* (Republic 1938), the hero was a mystery man who turned out to be one of the suspects pictured here: Lane Chandler, Lee Powell, Herman Brix (later Bruce Bennett), Georg Letz (later George Montgomery) and Hal Taliaferro (formerly Wally Wales). That's Chief Thundercloud playing Tonto.

left: Deadwood Dick (Columbia 1940) wa another popular pulp folk-hero. Don Douglas, a relatively unlikely choice for a serial hero, was surprisingly good in the title role. Assisting him in this scene was Lorna Gray, who shortly after moved to Republic and portrayed a wide variety of evil women under that screen name before changing it to Adrian Booth in the late forties.

9. A Stock Company of Villains

I HAVE DEDICATED THIS BOOK to the memory of the popular serial villain, Roy Barcroft (1902–69), the epitome of the stereotyped badman. Usually wearing a moustache, Barcroft could be equally satisfactory playing either the "brains" or "action" heavy. He schemed and fought his way through hundreds of B-Westerns and over twenty-five serials. He frankly admits modeling his screen characterizations after those of that popular Western villain of the thirties, Harry Woods, and he was able to surpass Woods in popularity during the forties. He made his first serial appearance in *Dick Tracy* in 1937 and free-lanced at various studios until 1943, when he signed a ten-year exclusive contract with Republic. Whatever amount of money he received was well-earned, for in those pre-union days contract players were forced to work back-breaking sixteen-hour days.

It seems rather incongruous that, off-screen, the king of villainy was one of the most beloved and respected members of the Republic acting roster, while many of the heroes turned out to be much less than the gentlemen they appeared to be on the screen. I recall spending a wonderful afternoon in early 1966 with Barcroft discussing serials, and I found that he, unlike so many of the people with whom he worked, loved doing them. He attributed this directly to the Republic stock company of players, who somehow made the tedious job of motion picture acting *fun*—men like Bud Geary, LeRoy Mason, George J. Lewis, and Kenne Duncan. The heroes came for their two or three weeks of work, but those villains were there every day throughout the year, and for Roy Barcroft that made his work a pleasure.

Barcroft's favorite serial role was that of Captain Mephisto in *Manhunt of Mystery Island,* a 1945 Republic action-thriller, but he enjoyed *The Purple Monster Strikes* and *Haunted Harbor* almost as much.

Charles Middleton's film career spanned many years and hundreds of roles, yet he is best remembered for one serial role. As Ming the Merciless in *Flash Gordon, Flash Gordon's Trip to Mars,* and *Flash Gordon Conquers the Universe,* he brought new dimension to screen villainy. How many serial fans could ever forget Buster Crabbe's repeated warnings to Middleton to "keep his slimy hands off" Jean Rogers (as Dale Arden)? The role of the despotic emperor was perfectly cast, and Middleton overacted to perfection. Though these Universal films may have been the main course, his superb portrayals of Pa Stark in *Dick Tracy Returns* and 39013 in *Daredevils of the Red Circle* were additional morsels of screen chicanery serial-watchers could relish.

Anthony Warde very likely holds the record

for appearing in more screen fights than any other "action" heavy save only Roy Barcroft. Allan Lane belted him around in *King of the Mounties*, Tom Steele really mauled him in *The Masked Marvel*, Larry Thompson pummeled him in *King of the Forest Rangers*, Bruce Edwards tried to teach him the error of his ways in *The Black Widow*, Kirk Alyn gave him a great going-over in *Radar Patrol vs. Spy King*, and Jim Bannon knocked him clear across the border in *Dangers of the Canadian Mounted*. Could any villain ask for more? And that was just at Republic. Over at Universal he was also Killer Kane, Buck Rogers' number-one adversary.

I have mentioned "brains" and "action" heavy several times. I really should clarify these terms before we proceed any further. The "brains" heavy was the man (or, on occasion, woman) who issued the orders to his henchmen. He usually had little to do until the last chapter except talk, snarl, or grimace. The "action" heavy or heavies went from one chapter to the next trying desperately to kill the hero with fists, knives, guns, bombs or whatever else happened to be handy at the time.

George J. Lewis was an expert at playing both types of roles. As Lionel Atwill's chief henchman, Matson, in *Captain America*, he had the unique distinction of being killed in chapter eleven and brought "back to life" by a miraculous machine, only to be killed again a few chapters later. In *G-Men vs. The Black Dragon* he looked like a fugitive from a tong war as he tried desperately to deprive the United States of the services of Rod Cameron, and in *Federal Operator 99* he tried to convince viewers that he was a gentle "brains" heavy by periodically playing the "Moonlight Sonata" on the piano while he sent Hal Taliaferro out to do his dirty work. Republic did try to convert George, though, by allowing him to assist lovely Linda Stirling in *Zorro's Black Whip*. It was the first time he had played a serial hero since the early days of Mascot when he had starred in *The Wolf Dog* with Rin-Tin-Tin.

In silent serials there was a particular fascination for Oriental villains. The "Yellow Peril" was constantly menacing "our American Way of Life." Warner Oland played this Asian stereo-type to perfection. When the sound serial thrived in the thirties, the task of portraying non-Caucasian menaces usually fell to Frank Lackteen. But of all his many and varied roles, the one fans most prefer is his portrayal of Shamba, the evil witch doctor in *Jungle Girl*. What a going-over he gave poor Frances Gifford: poison-gas-filled rooms, sacrificial altars, spear-traps, a room in which the floor slid back to reveal an apparently bottomless black abyss, and other assorted nastinesses that would have caused a lesser heroine to collapse from pure fatigue. Years later Republic was to make a feature called *Daughter of the Jungle,* utilizing stock footage from this serial. Lackteen was brought back to shoot additional scenes, and he seemingly hadn't aged at all.

And, of course, mention must be made of at least two ladies who could dish out their own brand of alluring devilment: Lorna Gray and Carol Forman. As the evil Vultura, Lorna actually stole the acting honors from serial queen Kay Aldridge in *Perils of Nyoka*. However, it must be noted that she had the help of Satan, the wildest gorilla since King Kong, while all Kay had was Clayton Moore. In later years Lorna Gray changed her name to Adrian Booth, and became Monte Hale's favorite leading lady. She could have remained malicious for a few more serials, if only to give Roy Barcroft a rest from overwork. A few years later, however, Carol Forman arrived on the scene and began to weave her evil webs as the Spider Lady in Columbia's first *Superman* serial, and over at Republic as *The Black Widow*. She was superb—and she was sexy. What more could one ask for?

And there were so many others! Especially Charles King, the rotund star of so many Westerns and serials; and Kenne Duncan, who, after faithfully serving Roy Barcroft for fifteen action-packed episodes of *Haunted Harbor*, was rewarded with a bullet simply because he knew Roy's real identity; and LeRoy Mason, Bud Geary, Hal Taliaferro, Ted Adams, George Cheseboro, Tom London, Stanley Price, William Haade, Robert Frazer, and Tristram Coffin. They deserve our thanks for making so many heroes look so much better than they really were.

left: LeRoy Mason was equally villainous in Westerns and non-Westerns such as *Daughter of Don Q* (Republic 1946). *below:* Kenne Duncan made hundreds of Westerns and serials, almost always as the villain. In this portrait from *The Adventures of Captain Marvel* (Republic 1941), he was the Scorpion's right-hand man.

left: John Merton departed from his usual Western villainy from time to time to portray mad scientists such as Dr. Tymak in *Brick Bradford* (Columbia 1947). *below, left:* The most famous of all serial villains, character-wise, was Ming the Merciless, portrayed by Charles Middleton in the three Flash Gordon serials. This portrait is from the first of the triology, *Flash Gordon* (Universal 1936). *below, right:* George J. Lewis could play heroes (*Zorro's Black Whip* [Republic 1944] assisting Linda Stirling), but was much better cast as the heavy in serials such as, here, *Federal Operator* 99 (Republic 1945).

right: Charles King was everybody's favorite villain in serials and Westerns during the thirties and forties. This portrait is from the Tom Mix serial, *The Miracle Rider* (Mascot 1935). *below, left:* Anthony Warde was often used as the main "action" heavy at Republic, but he is probably best remembered for playing Killer Kane in *Buck Rogers* (Universal 1939). This portrait is from *The Masked Marvel* (Republic 1943). *below, right:* Bud Geary, here in *Haunted Harbor* (Republic 1944), usually played "action" heavies superbly.

Frank Lackteen's broad foreign accent made him a natural serial villain. In *Jungle Girl* (Republic 1941) he portrayed Shamba, the evil witch doctor who menaced Frances Gifford.

above: Here in another still from *The Miracle Rider* (Mascot 1935) is Tom London, whose career of portraying good guys and bad guys spanned virtually the entire range of serial production, silent and sound. *left:* John Davidson delighted serial fans as the villainous Lucifer in *Dick Tracy vs. Crime Inc.* (Republic 1941) and Gruber in *Captain America* (Republic 1943), but he could play sympathetic roles with equal skill, such as Tal Chotali in *Adventures of Captain Marvel* (Republic 1941). *below:* Carleton Young specialized in superb character roles, many of them villainous. In *Dick Tracy* (Republic 1937) Young portrayed Ralph Byrd's brother after the mysterious Lame One had performed one of his "operations" to convert him from good guy to bad guy.

Tristram Coffin was usually the "brains" heavy who sent out a parcel of henchmen to attack the hero. Although he did portray one serial hero, Jeff King in *King of the Rocket Men* (Republic 1949), he was much more successful in villainous roles.

Hal Taliaferro changed his name from Wally Wales, which had been his name tag as a Western hero, and became one of the screen's better Western and non-Western villains. In *Federal Operator 99* (Republic 1945) he was George J. Lewis' right-hand man.

above: John Piccori specialized in portraying demented associates of the lead villain in serials like *Dick Tracy* (Republic 1937), *above,* and *Fighting Devil Dogs* (Republic 1938). *left:* Bob Kortman was another Western and Indian specialist in screen villainy. In *The Miracle Rider* (Mascot 1935) he opposed Tom Mix.

Naturally, there were screen villainesses too. Carol Forman was among the
best of these distaff devils, here portraying the title role in *The Black
Widow* (Republic 1947).

Buster Crabbe in *Tarzan, the Fearless* (Principal 1933), the first of his nine starring serials.

90

10. The Serial Heroes

IN DON SHAY's recently published book of film personality interviews, *Conversations*, Buster Crabbe is quoted as saying: "Actually I think I was kind of an uninteresting person. There was never any glamour for me in the picture business. There *is* a certain amount of satisfaction in having people recognize you, but I've never had anybody pass me in the lobby—you can hear people talk; some of them are extra loud—and say: 'There goes Buster Crabbe, the actor.' Nine times out of ten: 'There goes Buster Crabbe, the swimmer.'"

Most serial filmgoers would disagree. For them he was Flash Gordon, Buck Rogers, Red Barry, Tarzan, Captain Silver, the Mighty Thunda. He was all of these and more. As Pearl White was the chief performer linked with silent serials, so was Buster Crabbe the name most closely associated with the sound serial. There is no question that he was the most popular serial star of the golden age of sound serials, starring in nine episodic delights: *Tarzan, the Fearless, Flash Gordon, Flash Gordon's Trip to Mars, Red Barry, Buck Rogers, Flash Gordon Conquers the Universe, The Sea Hound, Pirates of the High Seas,* and *King of the Congo.* The reason for his serial success was obvious: he was handsome, with a good build, spoke dialogue with a reasonable amount of conviction, and could perform most of the routine action demanded of a perfect hero. What more was needed?

If Republic personnel had been asked what their requirements for a serial hero would be, one would most likely hear: "that the lead very closely resemble one of the stunt men on the studio payroll." That no doubt accounted for some of the rather routine leads they frequently used. But there were a number of actors who did their serial duty in a most creditable fashion.

Tom Tyler, mostly remembered as a Western player, was an excellent choice to play leads in a variety of serials, including *Phantom of the West, Jungle Mystery, Clancy of the Mounted,* and *The Phantom.* Tyler, like Crabbe, was a superb athlete and a physically perfect choice to play super heroes. A minor handicap, however, was his voice, which many found not on a par with his other attributes. It seems a rather strange coincidence that in his most famous serial, *The Adventures of Captain Marvel,* he spoke the equivalent of only one full page of dialogue in the entire twelve chapters. His one long speech, delivered at the end of the serial, seemed almost beyond his capabilities. Despite that flaw, he was one of the all-time serial favorites.

Once cast as Dick Tracy, Ralph Byrd was to remain Dick Tracy for the remainder of his screen career. A very personable leading man, he was excellent in serials like *S.O.S. Coast Guard* and *Blake of Scotland Yard,* but when Republic cast him as the famous comic-strip detective in the 1937 production of *Dick Tracy* his acting fate was sealed. He made three very successful sequels, *Dick Tracy Returns* in 1938, *Dick Tracy's G-Men* in 1939, and *Dick Tracy vs. Crime, Inc.* in 1941. They were all excellent; with many enjoying best his bout with the Spider in the first, while others favored the last, which had him battling the invisible Ghost.

Clayton Moore had one of those strange up and down careers that found him playing both leading man and chief villain with equal success. His first starring role was as Kay Aldridge's defender through fifteen episodes of *Perils of Nyoka.* His future seemed secure at Republic, but World War II intervened, and he, like so many others, went into uniform. When he returned to the studio and serial work in 1946's *The Crimson Ghost,* it was as the "action" heavy opposing Charles Quigley and Linda Stirling. The next year he once again emerged as a leading hero in *Jesse James Rides Again* and followed that with *G-Men Never Forget, Adventures of Frank and Jesse James,* and *Ghost of Zorro*—before once again turning villainous in *Radar Men from the Moon.* In between these Republic parts, he had become television's Lone Ranger (a role he still plays today in personal appearances) and went to Columbia to appear in *Son of Geronimo* (billed as Clay Moore) and *Gunfighters of the Northwest.*

Kane Richmond, a leading man in a number of B-films, appeared to give more dimension to routine roles than the scripts demanded. Playing a dual role in *Spy Smasher,* he delivered an amazingly good portrayal of the comic-strip character in a thrill-packed action serial that had David Sharpe, doubling for Richmond, performing exceptional stunts. In *Haunted Harbor,* Kane had the able assistance of Kay Aldridge as he battled Roy Barcroft for fifteen episodes. Over at Columbia, the results were far less satisfactory. In *Brenda Starr, Reporter* he assisted Joan Woodbury through ridiculous Columbia contrivances; in *Jungle Raiders* the script was self-defeating, and *Brick Bradford* was a weak and uninspired production. Unfortunately, Kane retired from films much too early to satisfy the appetites of serial fans.

Kirk Alyn gained his reputation playing Superman in two serials at Columbia, but he was much better as a straight actor in favorites like *Daughter of Don Q, Radar Patrol vs. Spy King, Blackhawk,* and *Federal Agents vs. Underworld, Inc.*

Another popular action favorite was Allan Lane. Long before he became the Rocky Lane of Western fame (and the voice of television's famous horse, Mr. Ed) he had starred in four action-packed Republic adventures: *King of the Royal Mounted, King of the Mounties, Daredevils of the West,* and *The Tiger Woman* (Linda Stirling's first serial).

Lee Powell, who achieved star status in *The Lone Ranger* and *Fighting Devil Dogs,* might have become one of the most popular of leading men in serials if fate had not taken a hand—he was killed overseas during World War II when he fell victim to an enemy booby trap.

Few serial leading men ever used their roles as stepping stones to greater film glory, except for John Wayne, who had starred in *Hurricane Express, Shadow of the Eagle,* and *The Three Musketeers* for Mascot, and George Brent, who for the same studio had starred in *Lightning Warrior.* And, of course, Gene Autry became famous after his stint in *Phantom Empire.*

A great many excellent character actors did "lower" themselves from time to time to appear in serial roles, with mixed results. Gilbert Roland wasn't half bad in *The Desert Hawk;* Paul Kelly was successful in combating espionage as the Black Commando in *The Secret Code;* Victor Jory couldn't save *The Shadow* or *The Green Archer* from the ineptness of director, James V. Horne; and Jack Holt, who really looked more like Dick Tracy in the flesh, was *Holt of the Secret Service.*

And then there were the forgotten heroes who made a serial or two and then vanished because they just didn't have the stuff of which serial heroes are made. Among others there were: George Turner, Lewis Wilson, Robert Kellard, Robert Scott, Lee Roberts, Richard Bailey, Marten Lamont, Larry Thompson, and Bruce Edwards.

left: Buster Crabbe, the most famous and durable of all the great serial heroes, in *Flash Gordon's Trip to Mars* (Universal 1938). *below:* Buster Crabbe in a publicity still for *Flash Gordon* (Universal 1936).

right: Buster Crabbe in *Pirates of the High Seas* (Columbia 1950). *below:* Buster Crabbe in his final serial, *King of the Congo* (Columbia 1952).

above: Charles Quigley was an ideal type for a serial hero but was used very sparingly. *The Crimson Ghost* (Republic 1946) was his final starring serial. *left, above:* Clayton Moore ranked second to Buster Crabbe in the number of starring serials he appeared in. A very likable hero, he often appeared with equal success as a villain. This publicity still is from one of the best-remembered serials of the forties, *Perils of Nyoka* (Republic 1942). He later went on to much greater fame by becoming television's *Lone Ranger. left, below:* Allan Lane, although more famous as a Western hero in the late forties, was another pleasant and capable serial hero. He appeared in four of Republic's best action serials, the last of which was *The Tiger Woman* (Republic 1944), from which this portrait was taken.

top: Grant Withers, much better known for his note-worthy character work in features, was an excellent serial lead in such favorites as *Radio Patrol* (Universal 1937) and, here with Henry Brandon, *Jungle Jim* (Universal 1937). *above:* Lee Powell in *Fighting Devil Dogs* (Republic 1938). Powell might have been the greatest serial hero of them all if World War II had not come along. He was reported killed in action. *right:* Rod Cameron starred in two wartime action serials and then moved up the ladder to success in feature roles. This scene is one of the chapter endings from *G-Men vs. The Black Dragon* (Republic 1943).

Don Terry, more famous as Don Winslow in two later serials, was excellent in one of Columbia's few good serials, *The Secret of Treasure Island* (Columbia 1938).

Linda Stirling, Republic's most famous serial queen of the forties, in a portrait drawn by noted artist Gray Morrow.

11. ... and the Heroines

THE SERIAL HEROINE, who rose to majestic heights of popularity in silent films when stars like Pearl White, Ruth Roland, and Helen Holmes thrilled millions of moviegoers, fell quickly out of favor when the sound serial made its appearance. After all, the serials were now primarily made for young boys, and young boys *knew* that women were too fragile to engage in the strenuous activity demanded of a serial star. A heroine was necessary only as someone to be placed in peril, and as someone to be repeatedly hit over the head so that she would not be in the path of the hero's swinging fists. Her status was dismal, to say the least. However, during the thirties, there was some attempt to once again build a few of the ladies into interesting, if not active, co-stars. Universal tried—but failed—to re-establish the serial queen in a 1934 remake of *Perils of Pauline* starring Evalyn Knapp. Dorothy Gulliver and Lucile Browne made some screen impression over at Mascot, but their appeal was short-lived. The only woman who seemed to make it in the eyes of adventure fans was lovely Jean Rogers. As Dale Arden in *Flash Gordon* and *Flash Gordon's Trip to Mars*, Rogers was a delectable morsel to be pawed again and again by Ming the Merciless. The only problem seemed to be that she screamed and fainted

with alarming regularity, and that offset the teasing sensations she imparted to the youthful audience by wearing skimpy costumes. She was, however, an effective aide to John King in *Ace Drummond* and Don Briggs in *Adventures of Frank Merriwell*.

But it was Republic Pictures, as usual, who restored dignity to the weaker sex. In 1941 they acquired the services of beautiful Frances Gifford and presented her with the title role in *Jungle Girl*. She was the dream girl of that serial year as she braved all the perils evil Frank Lackteen and Gerald Mohr could place in her path. She was trapped in a flooded mine, sacrificed on a flaming altar, gassed, precipitated into a burning vat of oil, and in varying ways threatened with death for fifteen thrilling weeks, only to be rescued by her own ingenuity or the skill of hero Tom Neal at the appropriate last moment. She was scheduled, and announced, to play her *Jungle Girl* character Nyoka again in *Perils of Nyoka* the following year, but personal problems intervened and another casting choice was made.

Kay Aldridge had an accent you could cut with a knife, looked terrible in a poorly designed costume (whereas Gifford's outfit was ideal), and couldn't act well enough to deliver more than an adequate performance. Yet she became one of Republic's best-exploited and most-liked serial heroines, appearing in three of their best serials, *Perils of Nyoka*, *Daredevils of the West* and *Haunted Harbor*. True to the standard heroine's role, Kay received her full share of blows on the head and holds the dubious distinction of being knocked unconscious *twice* in a single episode of *Haunted Harbor*.

And then came Linda Stirling. In its continuing effort to re-establish the idea of the serial queen, Republic tested Linda for the leading role in *The Tiger Woman*. Linda recalled that it was Yakima Canutt who directed her audition, which required her to ride a horse full tilt at the camera and rein up suddenly. According to her, "the horse stopped, but I didn't," and the young Linda Stirling practically fell in Canutt's lap. But the studio was happy with the test, and she got the role of the Tiger Woman, and followed it with leading roles in *Zorro's Black Whip*, *Manhunt of Mystery Island*, *The Purple Monster Strikes*, *The Crimson Ghost*, and *Jesse James Rides Again*. In addition to being the most beautiful of the Republic heroines (she had a very successful modeling career before coming to Republic), she could *act!* Those who viewed the serials when they were originally released looked at them with a certain amount of respect and admiration, but cared little for the effort that went into making them. Today movie buffs regard the serials with considerably more reverence than the people who made them. For example, Linda can only recall that they were a lot of work, great fun, and occasionally quite dangerous. While she was doubled in many instances, she did nearly drown in a sequence for *The Purple Monster Strikes* and narrowly escaped a dangerous fall—she was saved by stunt man Tom Steele—in *Manhunt of Mystery Island*. In filming serials there is always a certain element of risk. Fortunately, Linda Stirling and most of the others survived the perils of making films filled with perils.

There were other females who assisted their male companions with some degree of skill and enthusiasm. Peggy Stewart was excellent in Westerns like *The Phantom Rider* and *Son of Zorro*. Noel Neill of the childlike voice and appearance was ideal as Lois Lane in the two Superman serials, but she seemed miscast as a frontier heroine in *Adventures of Frank and Jesse James*. Helen Talbot was effective in *Federal Operator 99* and *King of the Forest Rangers*. Lorna Gray, when she wasn't playing a villainess in vehicles like *Perils of Nyoka* and *Federal Operator 99*, did take a fling at good-girl roles in *Captain America*, *Flying G-Men*, *Deadwood Dick*, and, under the name of Adrian Booth, *Daughter of Don Q.* Iris Meredith was a favorite over at Columbia in *The Spider's Web*, *Overland with Kit Carson*, and *The Green Archer*.

Most of the girls made one or two serials and then vanished from the screen forever. Few remember Ella Neal, Lita Conway, Vivian Coe, Luana Walters, Sheila Darcy, and dozens of others who had one brief moment of screen glory and then departed for the safety of marriage and private life. Not many serial heroines ever gained more than casual notice from the A-film producers. Carole Landis did rise from *Daredevils of the Red Circle* to minor prominence in lesser Twentieth Century-Fox films, and Jinx Falken of *The Lone Ranger Rides Again* became more famous by adding a "berg" to her last name, but the only one to really gain the top was young Phylis Isley of *Dick Tracy's G-Men;* she was discovered by David O. Selznick and changed her name to Jennifer Jones. There were, however, quite a number of B-film greats who took time off from busy schedules to make an occasional chapter play: Joan Woodbury, Adele Jergens, Veda Ann Borg, Anne Nagel, Phyllis Coates, Jane Adams, Evelyn Brent, Joyce Bryant, Ramsay Ames, Jennifer Holt, and Elyse Knox, to name only a few.

At the time, perhaps all of these gals seemed more a hindrance than a help to the serials' action, but it was still nice to have them around.

After many years of male domination in the serial field, Republic tried to bring back the serial queen in the exciting *Jungle Girl* (Republic 1941), starring the beautiful, and talented, Frances Gifford.

Adrian Booth was famous for playing outstanding villainess roles such as Vultura in *Perils of Nyoka* (Republic 1942) under her screen name of Lorna Gray. Under her new name she became a favorite Republic heroine in Westerns and serials such as *Daughter of Don Q* (Republic 1946), in which she appears here with Roy Barcroft and George Chesebro.

right: Linda Stirling had first-rate assistance from Allan Lane in *The Tiger Woman* (Republic 1944), the first of her six starring serials. *below:* Joan Woodbury was *Brenda Starr, Reporter* (Columbia 1945), a serial based on the famous comic strip. That's Wheeler Oakman, a popular serial villain in the '30s, with the gun.

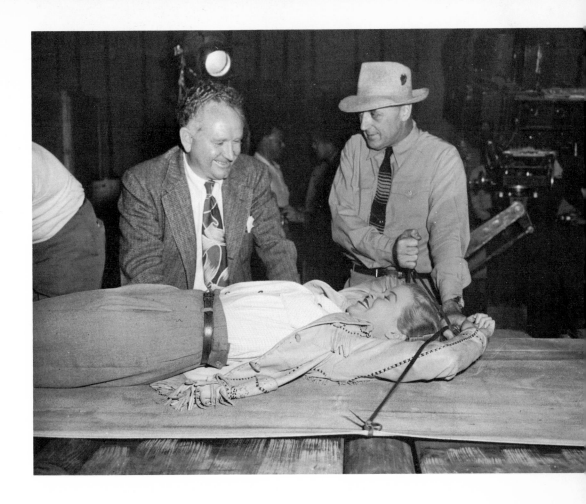

above: Spencer Gordon Bennet, the king of serial directors, shows fellow director Frank Borzage how serial heroine Helen Talbot should be bound in this production shot from *King of the Forest Rangers* (Republic 1946). *left:* Iris Meredith made a career out of screaming in Columbia serials. This time it's in *The Green Archer* (Columbia 1940).

Joyce Bryant almost became the victim of the grotesque villain in *The Iron Claw* (Columbia 1941).

left: Linda Stirling is about to learn the penalty for defying Roy Barcroft (as Captain Mephisto) and Kenne Duncan in the popular *Manhunt of Mystery Island* (Republic 1945). *below:* Pretty Peggy Stewart is being rescued by the masked hero, *The Phantom Rider* (Republic 1945).

Evalyn Knapp tried to bring back "poor Pauline" in the remake of *The Perils of Pauline* (Universal 1934). Hero Robert Allen rescues her, again, in this scene.

Second only to Linda Stirling in popularity among serial fans was Kay Aldridge, here facing one of the many *Perils of Nyoka* (Republic 1942).

Universal's claim to the serial-queen title was beautiful Jean Rogers, here seen as Dale Arden, with Buster Crabbe in *Flash Gordon* (Universal 1936).

Ruth Roman gives directions to Eddie Quillan and Edward Norris in *Jungle Queen* (Universal 1945).

12. Jungle Jeopardy

IT SEEMED RATHER a strange coincidence that both Republic and Columbia started off their serial production schedules with jungle films. *Darkest Africa,* Republic's first serial, released in early 1936, had Clyde Beatty, the famous animal trainer, as its star. Beatty had starred two years before in *The Lost Jungle* for Mascot, and he had proved to be a good box-office draw. Republic's serial was a wildly creative one, with Beatty fighting his way through the jungle to a lost city inhabited by, among many other things, a race of flying Bat Men. Accompanying Beatty, who could hardly be called an actor with any real skill, was Manuel King, a grotesque-looking young boy billed as the "World's Youngest Animal Trainer." There was plenty of stock from the earlier serial, and the film really achieved its only success in the extensive use of Howard Lydecker miniatures, including an erupting volcano at the film's climax. The flying sequences, done both with miniatures and with life-size dummies, were an excellent sampling of the superb effects later used in *The Adventures of Captain Marvel* and *King of the Rocket Men.*

Columbia, not to be outdone by Republic with their use of Beatty, obtained the services of a personality equally as important for their first serial, *Jungle Menace,* released in 1937. Frank Buck had already achieved considerable fame with his film documentary, *Bring 'Em Back Alive,* based on his own best-selling book detailing his capturing of animals for zoos all over the world. Buck, like Beatty, could hardly act his way out of a monkey cage, so what thrills there were in *Jungle Menace,* and there were very few "original" ones, were based mainly on antique stock jungle footage from the Columbia vaults. At least the supporting cast (Reginald Denny, Esther Ralston, LeRoy Mason, Charlotte Henry, and Duncan Renaldo, among others) gave more professional acting performances than Lucien Prival and his companions had delivered in *Darkest Africa.*

Most jungle serials were nothing more than glorified Westerns, usually shot on the same outdoor locations for much of their action, with close-ups being made on cheap studio sets decorated with imitation foliage. In order to spice up the proceedings, animal shots were inserted from stock libraries of various animals fighting each other or slinking around. Whenever the hero was required to fight an animal, he usually wound up with an obvious pet or a stuffed skin. There were exceptions, but they were rare. Herman Brix starred in *The New Adventures of Tarzan,* which actually was shot in Guatemala. Two of Republic's most famous jungle serials were almost entirely shot on the studio's back lot and Iverson's Ranch, the latter location being

111

one of the most-used locations in Western films and easily recognizable because of its rock formation resembling an Indian head.

Jungle Girl, which starred Frances Gifford as Nyoka, attempted to revive the serial-queen image absent from the screen for so many years. The plot was an interesting one. Nyoka's father is slain by his twin brother (both played by Trevor Bardette), who replaces him as a doctor serving the jungle tribes. Spurred on by the machinations of Slick Latimer (Gerald Mohr at his menacing best), the bogus doctor is trying to obtain a cache of diamonds hidden in the Caves of Nakros. With the treasure guarded by the evil witch doctor Shamba (played superbly by Frank Lackteen), it took fifteen thrill-packed episodes for Gifford, Tom Neal, and Eddie Acuff to dispose of all the opposition and rescue the diamonds. The ending of chapter one found Nyoka and Tom Neal trapped in one of the caves and Shamba flooding it, plunging them both to certain death out the opening in the side of a sheer cliff. Who wouldn't come back next week to see how they escaped—as of course they had?

Perils of Nyoka, starring Kay Aldridge as Nyoka (in a role originally intended for Gifford), had a group of scientists, assisted by Clayton Moore and the jungle girl, seeking the legendary Tablets of Hippocrates. These scriptures held the "medical secrets of the ancients," including a cure for cancer. The evil Vultura, played by Lorna Gray, kept sending her henchmen, including Charles "Ming the Merciless" Middleton, out to retrieve the Tablets and the accompanying treasure for herself. The only hint of a jungle in this serial was Satan, an incredibly designed ape who was Vultura's pet.

Although Linda Stirling was beautifully costumed as *The Tiger Woman* and was, supposedly, head of a jungle tribe, there was no sign of anything even faintly resembling a jungle in the entire serial. LeRoy Mason, the villain of the piece, was trying to acquire Linda's oil lands and a mysterious urn containing the secret of her real background, unknown even to her. On her side was dashing Allan Lane, who defended her against the repeated advances of George J. Lewis and others.

Call of the Savage, which had young Noah Beery, Jr., playing Jan of the Jungle, started out as a routine trek through the woods when suddenly in chapter ten a hidden city was revealed,

and Beery, aided by others in the cast, had a marvelous time being trapped in such elaborate devices as a room with descending spikes and a similar room whose floor slid back precipitating its occupants into a flaming abyss. Great fun for all!

More than ten years after *Perils of Nyoka,* Republic churned out an incredible cheapie called *Panther Girl of the Kongo,* which had Phyllis Coates, dressed exactly like Frances Gifford's *Jungle Girl* (for the purpose of matching shots), battling an army of so-called claw monsters who were terrorizing the jungle tribes. The monsters were nothing more than simple crayfish filmed against miniature sets created by Howard Lydecker and his special-effects department.

Ruth Roman, who delivered some quality performances in later years, was the mysterious *Jungle Queen* in Universal's 1945 wartime thriller. The plot of this creaking vehicle revolved around Nazis sending their agents into the (back lot) jungle to stir up the tribes to revolt against the Allies. Helping to keep the villains, led by Douglass Dumbrille, in check were Edward Norris and Eddie Quillan.

Lost City of the Jungle, topcasting Russell Hayden and Keye Luke, had Lionel Atwill playing the lead villain. Atwill died during the production of the film, and in order to complete the serial, shots of a very obvious double were used, photographing the replacement from behind. Then reaction shots of Atwill were spliced in at the appropriate time. Thus a cast member would be seen addressing Atwill in, say, a bar room, and his reaction shot would have Atwill standing in a completely different location. Also embarrassingly hilarious to watch was the matching of Hayden's and Luke's new footage with that of Jon Hall and Sabu from scenes taken from the earlier feature, *White Savage.* Footage from this earlier feature was utilized as chapter endings for at least three episodes. Universal certainly got their money's worth!

There were several other jungle serials of varying degrees of importance. Buster Crabbe was effective as the Lord of the Jungle in *Tarzan, the Fearless,* and not so potent as the Mighty Thunda in *King of the Congo;* Clayton Moore was seen completely at a disadvantage in *Jungle Drums of Africa,* which, almost everyone agrees, was the weakest of the sixty-six serials turned out by Republic; William Tracy and

Granville Owen tried valiantly to uncover the
secrets of a lost civilization in *Terry and the
Pirates* but only succeeded in finding viewers'
funny bones; and Tom Tyler roamed his jungle
kingdom in *The Phantom* with much less interest and enthusiasm than he had done many years
before when he had helped to solve the *Jungle
Mystery*.

On the whole, audiences were thankful that
the studios' forays into the jungle were of brief
duration.

right: Kay Aldridge represented Republic's second
attempt (Frances Gifford was the first) to bring
back the image of the serial queen. Her most famous
role was that of Nyoka in *Perils of Nyoka* (Republic
1942). *below:* Phyllis Coates (wearing an exact
duplicate of Frances Gifford's costume in *Jungle Girl*
[Republic 1941] for the matching of stock shots)
looks amazingly calm under the circumstances in
Panther Girl of the Kongo (Republic 1955).

above: Clyde Beatty, Cecilia Parker and Syd Saylor are interrupted by something, or someone, in *The Lost Jungle* (Mascot 1934).
left: Popular "Bring 'Em Back Alive" hunter Frank Buck was the star of Columbia's first serial, *Jungle Menace* (Columbia 1937).
below: Noah Berry, Jr., was Jan of the Jungle in *Call of the Savage* (Universal 1935). Harry Woods, usually a villain but this time cast as Jan's aide, seems to be having a bit of trouble with the snake.

right: Republic, like Columbia, also had a jungle serial as its initial serial offering. Clyde Beatty, here protecting Elaine Shepard, was the star of *Darkest Africa* (Republic 1936). *below:* Clayton Moore was the star of the dullest of all sixty-six Republic serials, *Jungle Drums of Africa* (Republic 1953).

above: Frances Gifford is about to be sacrificed on an elaborate altar which would propel her into a blazing inferno by witch doctor Shamba, played by Frank Lackteen in *Jungle Girl* (Republic 1941). *below:* Cecilia Parker is about to be saved from an unpleasant fate by Tom Tyler, Frank Lackteen, and Noah Berry, Jr., in *Jungle Mystery* (Universal 1932).

Herman Brix (later Bruce Bennett) was one of the best screen Tarzans in
The New Adventures of Tarzan (Burroughs-Tarzan 1935).

Richard Talmadge, one of the greatest of all stunt men, in a spectacular leap in his starring serial, *Pirate's Treasure* (Universal 1934).

118

13. The Stunt Men

THE MEN WHO *really* provided the major thrills and excitement in the serials were a small group of professional daredevils called stunt men, whose (planned) recklessness often left the viewing audience gasping in amazement.

During the days of the silent serial, many of the stars' reputations were based on the fact that they performed their own hazardous stunts. Joe Bonomo, Walter Miller, and Pearl White, among many others, seemed to flirt with death in every conceivable fashion as they went from one peril to another. However, as production costs rose, it became more apparent to producers that they could not risk injury to their star properties which might cause the shutdown of production on their films. Thus, a few select men who were willing to risk their lives for surprisingly little money began to travel from studio to studio doing yeoman service for countless leading men and women. Richard Talmadge, Cliff Lyons, and Yakima Canutt, in addition to Bonomo and Miller, formed the nucleus of the original stunt group.

Richard Talmadge was perhaps the most reckless of the group, and those who have seen some of his starring films like *The Speed Reporter*, *Never Too Late*, and his only starring serial, *Pirate's Treasure*, can only gasp in awe at some of the fantastic leaps he made time after time.

Cliff Lyons was an expert horseman and usually confined himself to doubling for cowboy stars like Buck Jones and Ken Maynard in their many features and serials. Rather heavy-set, Cliff was usually easy to spot when he was doing his action work. Talmadge, Lyons, and Yakima Canutt were all to become excellent second-unit directors in later years.

Yakima Canutt! During his heyday period of the twenties and thirties he doubled for so many people that he probably can't remember them all. A remarkable innovator, it was primarily Yakima who found safe ways to train animals to fall so that they wouldn't be injured, whereas formerly they were often brutally maimed and killed to please producers and directors who wanted thrills at any cost. He also helped bring the well-staged screen fight into being, teaching such Western stalwarts as John Wayne and Johnny Mack Brown how to throw a punch and make it look real. And all real action fans recall with admiration Yakima's specialty of jumping from a stagecoach to the lead horses, falling to the ground, letting the horses and coach pass over him and then catching on to the rear of the coach and climbing aboard again. A quite remarkable man!

As the serials grew in popularity in the thirties and forties, a new crop of eager young men entered the field. Tom Steele had a career which covered duty at Mascot, Universal, Columbia, and Republic, spanning almost the entire serial-producing years. Tom, who could handle almost all stunt specialties, was the head of the Republic staff for close to ten years and doubled almost all of the serial leads, as well as the B-Western leads, during those exciting years of the forties. Still active (he drove one of the cars in that amazing chase sequence in *Bullitt*), Tom looks about twenty years younger than he really is. Constantly on the lookout for new ways to bring honor and distinction to his field, he was one of the founders of the Stunt Men's Association. Tom has the unique distinction of having starred in a film almost as long as *Gone with the Wind* in running time and having received *no* screen credit whatsoever. When Republic made their action classic *The Masked Marvel*, Tom played the hero behind the mask, as well as a villain in a later chapter, and doubled in numerous fight sequences for the other leads, and yet his name never appeared on the screen. It seemed a little unfair, especially since the script was written specifically for him. Such are the ways of Hollywood.

Ask any stunt man who *his* favorite stunt man is and chances are that nine out of ten of them will answer David Sharpe. Sharpe, a superb athlete who specialized in tumbling, has also had a career almost equal in duration to that of Steele. Even though he was relatively short, he was often required to double tall leads like Tom Tyler, Allan Lane, and Kane Richmond. His work at Republic always included spectacular leaps from balconies and acrobatically staged fights in which he would do backflips and assorted other tricks that would have us all standing up and shouting in the aisles. In *The Adventures of Captain Marvel*, in which he doubled for Tom Tyler as the comic-strip hero, Sharpe's flying leaps were so superb that after a while you began to think that the Captain really *could* fly. On a panel show Sharpe was once asked if he had ever done any really dangerous stunts. His reply was no. He continued, "I would never do any stunt that I felt I was not physically capable of performing safely." But even Sharpe could miscalculate once in a great while. For a scene in *Spy Smasher* he was required to stage a spectacular forty-foot leap from a building, which was to blow up in miniature on the screen, to a parked truck. However,

he had not calculated on a heavy wind the day the scene was shot, and, because he was required to wear a cape in the role, which acted as a sail, he almost missed his target. Sharpe, like Steele, is still very active today, and you can find him still leaping off balconies (doubling for Tony Curtis in *The Great Race*) or, dressed like a little old lady, doing somersaults on the *Red Skelton* television show.

Dale Van Sickel was another popular favorite at Republic in the forties. His spectacular fight sequences with Tom Steele are classics. Van Sickel, a little heavier set than Steele, was an All-American football player prior to his film chores. Fast-paced action was routine when Van Sickel played the lead in *Captain America*, doubling for Dick Purcell, or *The Crimson Ghost*, in which he so closely resembled Charles Quigley, who was the star. One of Van Sickel's specialties is stunt driving, and his acrobatic car work for films like *On the Beach* is truly remarkable. Dale had a little stronger acting voice than many of his co-workers, so he is often seen playing character roles in Westerns and serials as well as performing stunt duty.

Eddie Parker was a veritable work-horse at Universal and was kept busy on all phases of their film production. It was Parker and Alan Pomeroy who doubled for Randolph Scott and John Wayne in that spectacular fight sequence in *The Spoilers*. At Republic, Parker could be found in at least one fight sequence per serial released during the forties. It seemed rather sad that, after all the incredible stunt work he had done in films, he was to succumb to a heart attack after working with Ken Terrell on a short fight routine for a Jack Benny television show.

Another tragedy was the accidental death of young Jimmy Fawcett, killed when he was struck by an automobile driven by actor Ralf Harolde. He resembled Sharpe physically, and many feel he would have been one of the top in the field, but his career lasted only a few short years in the late thirties and early forties.

And there are so many more who deserve mention: Duke Green, known affectionately as "Crazy Duke" because of his apparently reckless leaps from desk tops or whatever else happened to be available at the time; Ken Terrell, with his acrobatically staged fights; Fred Graham, who frequently took time off from doubling John Wayne in order to be battered around Republic sets; and, among others, Johnny Dahiem, Harvey Parry, Joe Yrigoyen, Carey Loftin, Ted Mapes, Reed Howes, and Duke Taylor.

These men deserve thanks for every one of those thousands of Days of Thrills and Adventure.

st-working of all serial stunt men was probably Tom Steele. Appearing , Universal, and Columbia serials, his most famous work was over at where he appeared in virtually every serial (and hundreds of Westerns es) made from the early forties to Republic's demise in 1955. Usually or the lead, Tom made frequent appearances in various episodes of and also as the main villain's henchman. His fight sequences with nt man Dale Van Sickel are action classics. Here Tom doubles for owers in *Desperadoes of the West* (Republic 1950).

Tom Steele

Tom Steele doubling for Rod Cameron in *Secret Service in Darkest Africa* (Republic 1943).

Dale Van Sickel

Another versatile action double was the talented Dale Van Sickel. Equally adept at fights, motorcycle work, and car chases, Dale helped give Republic its distinctive action style in the forties. In this scene from *The Crimson Ghost* (Republic 1946), Dale, doubling for Charles Quigley, runs up the wall in a spectacular fight sequence with Tom Steele doubling for Clayton Moore. Quite often the stunt men themselves devised these gags to provide variety.

Dale Van Sickel, doubling for Dick Purcell in *Captain America* (Republic 1943), delivers quite a punch to Ken Terrell. Note the band around Ken's neck holding his hat on.

David Sharpe

David Sharpe was an all-around athlete and specialized in tumbling, and his stunt work was filled with elaborate leaps and somersaults. Although he was relatively short, he doubled tall leads such as Tom Tyler and Kane Richmond so well that the youthful serial audience never noticed the difference. In this sequence Sharpe doubles for Don "Red" Barry in *Adventures of Red Ryder* (Republic 1940).

above: After a spectacular fight sequence, Sharpe, doubling for Kane Richmond in *Spy Smasher* (Republic 1942) does one of his specialties. *below:* David Sharpe doubling for Robert Wilcox as the Copperhead in *Mysterious Dr. Satan* (Republic 1940).

below: David Sharpe doubling for Tom Tyler in *The Adventures of Captain Marvel* (Republic 1941). *opposite page, above:* David Sharpe doubling for Ralph Byrd in *Dick Tracy vs. Crime, Inc.* (Republic 1941). *opposite page, below:* David Sharpe was occasionally called upon to double heroines because of his size. In *Perils of Nyoka* (Republic 1942) he performed many of the action stunts for star Kay Aldridge.

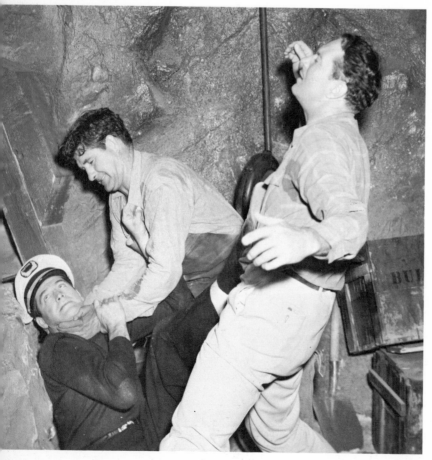

above: When Allan Lane and Linda Stirling faced Cliff Lyons, Duke Green, and Eddie Parker in *The Tiger Woman* (Republic 1944), you knew a tremendous fight sequence was due any moment. *left:* In the last chapter of *Haunted Harbor* (Republic 1944), Kane Richmond, doubled in the long shots by Dale Van Sickel, battles Fred Graham (*center*) and Eddie Parker, doubling for Roy Barcroft.

Yakima Canutt

right: Yakima Canutt is considered the dean of all action stunt men. A tremendous innovator, he went on to become a great second-unit director in later years. In this scene he does a transfer doubling for John Carroll in *Zorro Rides Again* (Republic 1937). *below:* A great deal more adept at stunting than acting, Yakima nevertheless played countless Western villains and minor roles, such as one of the "mole men" menacing Gwen Gaze in *The Secret of Treasure Island* (Columbia 1938).

Most early serial fights were wildly swinging brawls with little technique or form. Yakima helped fashion the well-staged fight which emerged in the late thirties. In this scene from *The Clutching Hand* (Weiss-Mintz 1936), Yakima is about to throw his opponent to the deck. That's Jack Mulhall playing Craig Kennedy, putting a stranglehold on "Bull" Montana.

14. World War II

REPUBLIC, BEST-EQUIPPED of the serial-producing companies to handle wartime "destruction" scenes on the screen because of their superb special-effects department, devoted five of their seven serials produced during 1942 and 1943 to the subject of fighting the common foe. After that, apparently tiring of the subject, none of the remaining seven serials produced during the war years of 1944 and 1945 had anything to do with the war.

Spy Smasher had hero Kane Richmond, playing twin brothers, opposing a typically hard-faced Nazi, Hans Schumm, called the Mask. Head of a spy ring in America, the Mask was thwarted time and time again as he tried to wreck planes, steal bombsights, and otherwise hinder our campaign against Germany. One particularly exciting chapter climax had Kane Richmond trapped and fleeing through a tunnel on a handcar while flaming oil rushed menacingly behind him. The Mask met a spectacular finish when his escaping submarine hit an Allied mine. One of the requisites of wartime serials was "self-sacrifice," and in *Spy Smasher* both the hero's brother and his closest friend, a French-man named Durand, willingly gave up their lives to save that of the spy fighter.

King of the Mounties could claim the distinction of having its hero (Allan Lane playing Sergeant King) battle representatives of all three Axis powers at the same time. Howard Lydecker created a spectacularly effective miniature volcano which the villains entered by means of a minature "bat plane." For a rousing finale, Sergeant King battled the enemy agents inside the volcano, accidentally knocking some stored bombs into the bubbling lava of the inert monster. Escaping via the "bat plane," he was just able to leave the vicinity of the volcano as the whole mountain erupted in an orgy of destruction. Many years later Republic was to use stock shots of this miniature for the hideout of the *Flying Disc Man from Mars*, and it was laughable to see the mock-up of the spaceship still emblazoned with the "Rising Sun" emblem.

Rod Cameron, playing Rex Bennett, starred in two of the most "explosive" action serials that Republic ever created. Each was filled with complex Lydecker miniatures that erupted in multiple bursts of billowing flame at the end of every episode, or so it seemed. In *G-Men vs. The Black Dragon*, Cameron battled the evil Japanese agent Haruchi, played with appropriate squint-eyed intrigue by Nino Pipitone, who had been smuggled into the United States in a mummy case after he had taken a drug that put him in a state of suspended animation. He too was destroyed when his explosive-laden speedboat crashed into a waiting submarine, sending both man and motorboat a blazing finale.

Having disposed of the Japanese, Cameron took on the Nazis in another part of the world in *Secret Service in Darkest Africa*. In this action-packed epic, Baron Von Rommler, played by Lionel Royce, captured and took the place of his look-alike, our African ally, Sultan Abou Ben Ali (Royce, again). It took Cameron fifteen episodes and about forty choreographed slugfests to finally uncover the truth and reward the Baron's villainy with death.

The Masked Marvel, an exciting hero, was in reality one of four insurance investigators who were on the trail of the infamous Sakima, a Japanese agent (portrayed by one-time comic-foil Johnny Arthur) bent on destroying our vital war industries. The role had been specifically written to utilize the services of Tom Steele, the head of the Republic serial stunt team. The action sequences were first rate, and once again the special effects dazzled the eye. Sakima met his death in almost a comic fashion. After a gun fight in which the Marvel emptied his gun at the cowering agent, Sakima announced gleefully, "*Your* bullets are all gone, but I still have *one* left." He rose to fire point-blank at the Marvel, only to be felled by another bullet from the masked man's gun. "Did it not occur to your Oriental mind," he proclaimed, "that I might *reload?*" I guess it didn't!

Over at Universal they were fighting the war on a cheaper level. Not possessing a very satisfactory special-effects department, they relied a great deal on integrating newsreel and other stock footage with cheaply done studio interiors. The results were poor, and too many minutes of valuable screen time were wasted. Don Terry was an effective lead in the title role of *Don Winslow of the Navy* and, a year later, *Don Winslow of the Coast Guard*. In both serials he battled a Nazi menace called the Scorpion, who was out to destroy our nation's defenses. A very young Lloyd Bridges also tackled the Nazis in *Secret Agent X-9*, and The Dead End Kids and

The Little Tough Guys took on the enemy in *Sea Raiders* and *Junior G-Men of the Air*. *Adventures of the Flying Cadets* had a bigger budget and managed to be fairly interesting. Combating a mysterious masked villain, the Black Hangman, heroes Johnny Downs and Bobby Jordan portrayed serial protagonists youthful fans could identify with.

Meanwhile, at Columbia they were also carrying on in a somewhat inept fashion, trying to turn out satisfactory serials on a minimal budget and, for the most part, steering clear of war propaganda. The two big exceptions were *The Batman* and *The Secret Code*. *The Batman*, based on the popular comic-strip character, had its masked hero pitted against the evil Japanese agent, Dr. Daka, played for full laugh value by the talented J. Carrol Naish. Its aim sabotage, the laboratory of Dr. Daka was a veritable treasure trove of scientific weapons and devices, including a helmet to convert men into walking zombies and special electrical equipment to bring the dead back to life. On a more pedestrian level, under a trap door the doctor had a carefully prepared pit full of alligators in which he disposed of his unwanted "guests," and, unfortunately, into which he was himself precipitated when chapter fifteen came around.

The Secret Code had versatile performer Paul Kelly playing the masked Black Commando, who was on the trail of an enemy spy ring trying to get possession of a top-secret formula the United States had developed for manufacturing synthetic rubber. After fifteen thrill-packed (for Columbia, they were thrill-packed indeed) episodes, the villains were destroyed by the tried and true method of having their escaping submarine rammed and destroyed. One entertaining gimmick connected with the serial was the inclusion at the end of each chapter of a very short lecture and demonstration on the breaking of secret codes.

opposite page, above: George J. Lewis and Noel Cravat prepare to get Rod Cameron to divulge some defense secrets in *G-Men vs. The Black Dragon* (Republic 1943). This serial contained more of Howard Lydecker's fantastic explosive miniatures than any other Republic serial. *opposite page, below:* Paul Kelly was the Black Commando in the Columbia wartime thriller, *The Secret Code* (Columbia 1942). At the end of each episode the audience was given a short lecture on solving secret messages.

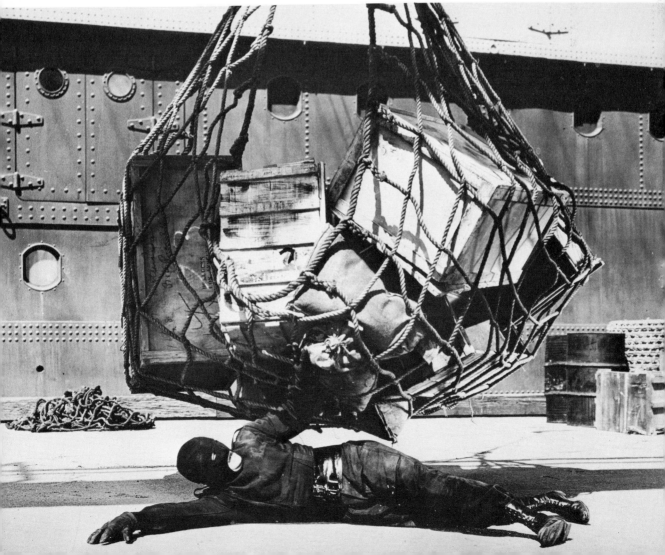

above: Don Terry was *Don Winslow of the Navy* (Universal 1942) and battled the Scorpion, a German bent on Allied destruction. *left:* The *Junior G-Men of the Air* (Universal 1942) fought enemy agents attempting to destroy American air power. In the cast were Frank Albertson, Bernard Punsly, Gabriel Dell, Huntz Hall, and Billy Halop.

right: Lloyd Bridges protects Jan Wiley from Nazi terrorists in *Secret Agent X-9* (Universal 1945). *below:* Allan Lane prepares to tackle Anthony Warde in *King of the Mounties* (Republic 1942). In this rousing epic, the villains were representatives of all three Axis powers: the Nazis, the Italians, and the Japanese. Their stronghold was inside a marvelous Howard Lydecker-constructed volcano, which erupted in a blazing screen finale.

Jack Holt looks as though he has everything well in hand as *Holt of the Secret Service* (Columbia 1941). It was a persistent fault of Columbia serials that they often portrayed a single hero fighting three or more villains at one time—and winning—thus turning the action sequences into comic-strip travesties.

15. They Got Their Men

WHENEVER THE STUDIOS wanted to add variety to their production schedules and still maintain relatively low production costs, they would make a non-Western Western by converting the hero from a fighting cowboy to a gallant Mountie. Aside from the change of costume and a change of location (instead of Iverson's Ranch, the film would probably be shot at Lone Pine, a few hours' drive from the studios), the films remained Western in flavor.

Republic fashioned several excellent screenplays to honor our Canadian neighbors, one of the most enjoyable being *King of the Royal Mounted*, released in 1940. Allan Lane, playing Sergeant King, was an ideal choice to portray the famous Zane Grey character, and the role marked the beginning of a long and rewarding association with the studio. He appeared in three additional serials and scores of Westerns. The action-packed story concerned itself with the discovery of a substance called compound X, which could cure infantile paralysis. Enemy agents found out that the same compound had certain magnetic properties which could make their mines effective against the British Navy. The entire film then dealt with the attempts by the agents to obtain quantities of the rare compound to ship to their government. The film was beautifully photographed, and David Sharpe, doubling in the action scenes for Lane, was in top form.

Two years later Lane starred in a sequel called *King of the Mounties*, which found him battling the Axis powers who were bent on sabotage in North America. Filled with more gimmicks, like a flying "bat plane," the serial was as exciting as the earlier entry.

The only other Mountie films turned out by the studio were 1948's *Dangers of the Canadian Mounted* and 1953's *Canadian Mounties vs. Atomic Invaders*. The former found Jim Bannon playing Christopher Royal on the trail of a gang headed by a mysterious Boss who was trying to locate the treasure of Genghis Khan, which turned out to be "liquid" diamonds which solidified when they were released from their ancient container; the latter found Bill Henry playing Sergeant Dan Roberts as he pursued enemy agents who were trying to establish missile sites from which they could launch an attack against North America. Both serials contained stock footage from the earlier Lane thrillers.

Universal and Columbia had managed to turn out a few serials starring the "Men in Red," but on the whole they were fairly routine actioners.

Tom Tyler was excellent in *Clancy of the Mounted* and Bill Kennedy was adequate in *The Royal Mounted Rides Again*, Universal's two entries in the field, while *Perils of the Royal Mounted*, starring Robert Kellard (billed now as Robert Stevens), *Gunfighters of the Northwest*, with Jack Mahoney (who went through several name changes), and *Perils of the Wilderness*, with Dennis Moore, did very little to cement American–Canadian relationships.

While serial makers were saluting our neighbors to the north, our own law-enforcement officials were helping to stamp out crime on the screen in a number of excellent screenplays. *Federal Operator 99* found Marten Lamont on the trail of the notorious Jim Belmont, a vicious criminal (expertly played by George J. Lewis) who, between various acts of villainy, liked to play the "Moonlight Sonata" on the piano. The finale of this serial was one of the most exciting ever filmed. The studio rented a deserted theatre in Hollywood, and director Spencer Bennet had his actors stage a beautifully photographed chase-and-fight sequence high above the stage in the fly area, from which the evil Belmont plunged to his death.

G-Men Never Forget gave veteran serial villain Roy Barcroft a chance to play a dual role. As the racketeer leader Murkland, Barcroft discovers his close resemblance to Commissioner Cameron. He kidnaps the policeman and assumes his identity to further his reign of terror. Clayton Moore, playing the hero, finally discovers the substitution and rescues the Commissioner. In a wild fight sequence, Barcroft as Cameron killed Barcroft's Murkland.

Our law officers in the South were guarding our security as well. "Slingin' Sammy" Baugh, the famous football star of the late thirties, deserted the gridiron, on film at any rate, to join the Texas Rangers when his Ranger father was mysteriously killed. The villain of the piece was Neil Hamilton, who was working for an unidentified alien power whose representative, referred to as His Excellency, hovered over the Texas plains in a dirigible giving instructions to his earthbound agents to sabotage vital industries. *King of the Texas Rangers*, released in 1941, was filled with spectacular special effects by Howard Lydecker, including a complete oil-field holocaust, the blowing-up of a dam, the wrecking of a tunnel while a train was passing through, and the grand finale which had

Baugh's plane plunging into the hovering dirigible, destroying the enemy agents in an exploding ball of flame.

In *Government Agents vs. Phantom Legion*, hero Walter Reed was combating a mystery man known simply as the Voice, who was bent upon disrupting the country's system of highway transportation; and in *Radar Patrol vs. Spy King*, Kirk Alyn had the task of tracking down the head of "the most dangerous ring of saboteurs in the annals of military intelligence," the evil Baroda. Both of these later Republic serials borrowed heavily from *G-Men vs. The Black Dragon* and other vintage material.

Even the United Nations found it needed help when a band of foreign agents began smuggling arms and munitions to subversive native groups in the Asian coastal country of Burmatra, where a revolution was being planned. Dispatched jiffy-quick to dispel these alien dreams of glory was Harry Lauter as *Trader Tom of the China Seas*. Of eleven chapter endings, only two were original for this serial; the remainder were taken from the earlier *Haunted Harbor*, *S.O.S. Coast Guard*, and *Drums of Fu Manchu*. Economy was indeed the word in those post-1948 serials.

And just to show audiences how important youngsters could be, Universal decided to let the Boy Scouts have their chance to help combat crime. In 1939's *Scouts to the Rescue*, young Jackie Cooper and his pals helped crack a counterfeiting ring operating in a deserted ghost town. Along the way they battled some rather offensive Indians who were trying to conceal a hidden cache of radium in their underground temple. It was excellent fun, and it gave the youthful viewers some heroes with whom they could more closely identify. Universal was to later utilize The Dead End Kids and The Little Tough Guys in future serials, such as *Sea Raiders* and *Junior G-Men of the Air*, for the same reason.

Also on the trail of counterfeiters was Jack Holt as *Holt of the Secret Service*, a Columbia release of 1941 which should have been better made. Unfortunately, Holt was just a little too old to engage in all the action, and kids could not really accept him.

No matter what the challenge may have been to our crime-fighters, the Allies always, somehow, managed to win. Whether it was opposing the Axis powers during World War II (*G-*

Men vs. The Black Dragon, Secret Service in Darkest Africa, etc.) or home-front racketeers Gang Busters, Secret Agent X-9, etc.), we sent our best-looking, most-qualified, strongest, and most durable leading men out to fight our battles. And in each and every instance, "they got their man."

right: Tom Tyler uncovers an important clue in *Clancy of the Mounted* (Universal 1933). *below:* In *Federal Agents vs. Underworld, Inc.* (Republic 1949), hero Kirk Alyn frequently tangled with Roy Barcroft and ace stunt man Tom Steele.

above: Allan Lane was a perfect choice to portray Sergeant King in the serial version of the popular comic strip *King of the Royal Mounted* (Republic 1940). This was the first of Lane's four serials for Republic. *below:* George Chesebro gets the drop on Robert Kellard in *Perils of the Royal Mounted* (Columbia 1942).

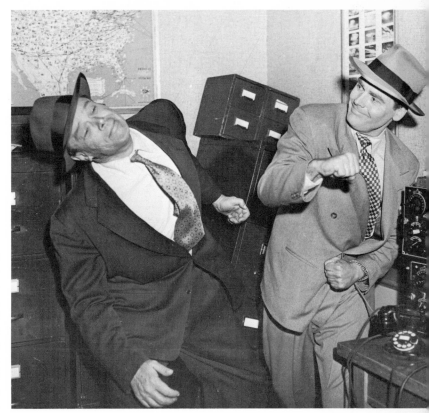

right: Walter Reed delivers a right cross to veteran villain Dick Curtis in *Government Agents vs. Phantom Legion* (Republic 1951). *below:* Harry Lauter, *second from right,* was a United Nations operative in *Trader Tom of the China Seas* (Republic 1954), assisted by Aline Towne as they uncover some villainy being planned by Fred Graham, *left,* and Tom Steele, two of Republic's best stunt men.

above: Jim Bannon thinks he has Anthony Warde under arrest, but stunt man Ken Terrell has other plans in this scene from *Dangers of the Canadian Mounties* (Republic 1948). *right:* Marten Lamont, who possessed a marked English accent, seemed a peculiar choice to play *Federal Operator 99* (Republic 1945), but he proved quite satisfactory. Ken Terrell gets the handcuff treatment in this scene from the film. *below:* Dale Van Sickel, a superb fight stunt man, takes one on the chin from Bill Henry in *Canadian Mounties vs. Atomic Invaders* (Republic 1953).

above: In *G-Men Never Forget* (Republic 1948) long-time villain Roy Barcroft, *left,* had a chance to play a dual role and ended the serial by killing his villainous counterpart. Aiding in discovering the deception were Clayton Moore and Ramsay Ames. *right:* Jack Mahoney, a first-rate stunt man, provided most of his own thrills in *Gunfighters of the Northwest* (Columbia 1954). *below:* Clayton Moore, this time on the wrong side of the law, tries to get information on the mysterious "cyclotrode" from Charles Quigley in *The Crimson Ghost* (Republic 1946).

The Scorpion was out to gain world domination by controlling the "golden scorpion atom-smasher" in *The Adventures of Captain Marvel* (Republic 1941).

16. Behind the Mask

THE SCORPION, the Ghost, the Octopus, the Wasp, the Lame One, the Spider, the Rattler, the Black Ace, the Dragon, the Mask, the Crimson Ghost, the Tiger Shark, Captain Mephisto, the Voice, the Eagle, Dr. Vulcan, and the Whispering Shadow . . .

What a magnificent collection, and only partial at that, of marvelous screen monstrosities!

If it was vitally important to the serial fan that the hero be the epitome of the "true-blue" good guy, it was no less important that the principal villain be depicted as evil incarnate. The appearance of a masked menace or mystery man, rather than the routine villain, was a time-tested hook for grabbing the interest of the youthful fan and bringing him back to the theatre week after week.

The concept of the mystery man was a simple theme with variations played over and over again. Usually there were three, four, or five men comprising a board of directors, or group of scientists, or staff of university professors, etc., one of whom led a villainous double life. Trying to guess which of the group was the guilty party was really a waste of time, for logical clues were seldom given to help you in making your decision. Your odds did increase, however, as the suspects in each particular group were gradually eliminated, usually by means of sudden and violent death, until only

two remained in the last chapter. And when the final denouement came, it was often a traumatic experience to find that, after fifteen weeks, you had guessed—*wrong!*

When it comes right down to picking a favorite among all these masters of menace, the choice usually narrows to two: the Lightning from the 1938 *Fighting Devil Dogs* and the Scorpion from the highly successful *The Adventures of Captain Marvel*, released in 1941.

The Lightning was indeed an imposing menace with his glistening black helmet and flowing cape. Possessing a deadly "electronic thunderbolt," he was systematically terrorizing the world by destroying ships, dirigibles, and entire communities. The assorted suspects included electronics specialists, a gardener, and a shifty-eyed butler. Quite naturally, the villain turned out to be the least obvious—or did he? The special effects of the Lightning's deadly attacks were spectacularly effective in helping to establish an aura of supreme evil.

But, as spectacular as the Lightning was, most serial aficionados are prone to accept the Scorpion as the more interesting villain. Perhaps the plot of *The Adventures of Captain Marvel* had more to do with this choice than the villain himself. A group of archaeologists travel to a remote region in Siam and there discover a tomb containing a mysterious "golden scorpion" containing five lenses which, when focused together, can create gold from ordinary rocks or, when placed in another position, can become one of the most deadly weapons known to man. The lenses are divided among the members of the expedition. That night the Scorpion, cloaked in a black mask and robe emblazoned with the emblem of the Scorpion dynasty, makes off with the skeleton of the deadly device, and the serial then moves into high gear as the sinister figure goes after the four lenses held by the remaining members of the party. When the final chapter unreels, all but one of the suspects has been violently disposed of. Captain Marvel exposes the Scorpion just in time to save the world, and the hooded figure is destroyed in the ray of the deadly machine, which is then, in turn, destroyed for all time.

A great factor in the success of the Scorpion's characterization was the use of Gerald Mohr's dubbed-in voice. This was a favorite cheat of the serial-makers. Since most of the suspects' voices would be readily identifiable, other voices were frequently used to the dismay of the attentive viewer. How boldly they cheated was best evidenced in *The Crimson Ghost*, in which they used I. Stanford Jolley's voice for the Crimson Ghost and, at the same time, included him in a scene in one of the later chapters in which he was quickly killed. Of course, there are always exceptions to the general rule: in *Dick Tracy vs. Crime, Inc.* the Ghost's voice actually belonged to the suspect involved.

Captain Mephisto in *Manhunt of Mystery Island* was one of the most intriguing of all serial mystery men. In this action-packed epic the hero (Richard Bailey) and heroine (Linda Stirling) travel to Mystery Island in search of the latter's father, the inventor of a "radiatomic transmitter"—another potentially "world-dominating" device. Of the four owner-suspects on the island, one is capable of placing himself in a strangely constructed chair and by turning on great electrical power is able to rearrange his molecular structure so that he emerges from the chair as a completely different personality—the reincarnation of an early pirate, Captain Mephisto (superbly played by Roy Barcroft in his favorite serial role). The bold pirate is holding the girl's father prisoner and is forcing him to build a more powerful and deadly machine. Before Mephisto meets his well-deserved end, the hero is almost put through the transformation in the hope that he will be mistaken for the pirate and killed.

The Ghost in *Dick Tracy vs. Crime, Inc.*, besides wearing a mask, had the additional advantage of having the ability to become invisible through the aid of a machine developed by his chief henchman, Lucifer. This gave the special-effects people at Republic a chance to utilize all kinds of visual tricks, and the final fight sequence in chapter fifteen is a masterpiece. In order to make the Ghost visible, Dick Tracy makes use of a special lamp bulb which, when turned on, emits infra red beams which reverse the polarity of the entire room and everything in it, exposing the arch-villain. This tremendous effect was achieved simply by printing the entire sequence in negative. The Ghost's demise was equally spectacular. Fleeing from Tracy, and still invisible, he attempts to escape by crossing high-tension wires. When the power switch is suddenly thrown on, the Ghost bursts into flame and plunges to the ground.

On and on they came. Dr. Vulcan with his "decimator" in *King of the Rocket Men*, *The Crimson Ghost* with his "cyclotrode," and all the others. They were evil, monstrous, power-mad devils, and they all met well-deserved ends —and audiences *loved* every one of them!

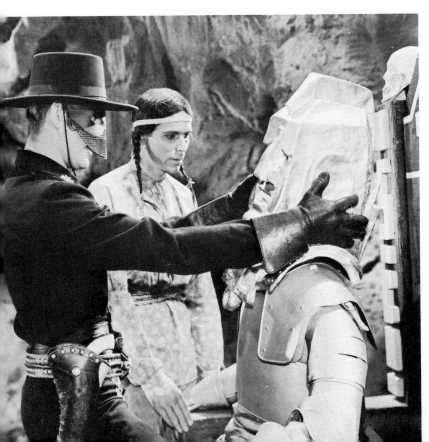

above: Batman and Robin (Columbia 1949) were out to discover who the Wizard was. *left:* Reed Hadley as Zorro and Paul Marian think they are about to unmask the mysterious Don Del Oro in *Zorro's Fighting Legion* (Republic 1939).

above: The Wasp finally meets Warren Hull as Mandrake face to face in *Mandrake the Magician* (Columbia 1939). *left: Dick Tracy* (Republic 1937) had to contend with this fellow, who went under the name of the Spider and the Lame One. *below:* Bob Steele is about to unmask the Black Ace in *Mystery Squadron* (Mascot 1933).

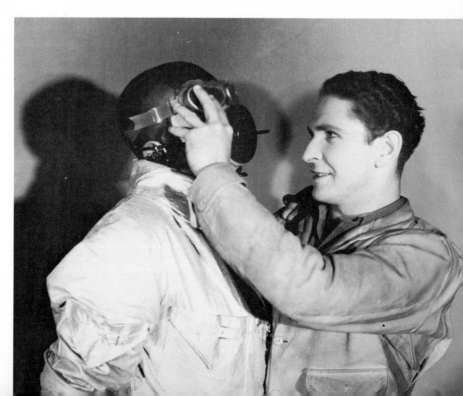

The villainous El Shaitan delivers orders to his men in *The Three Musketeers* (Mascot 1933).

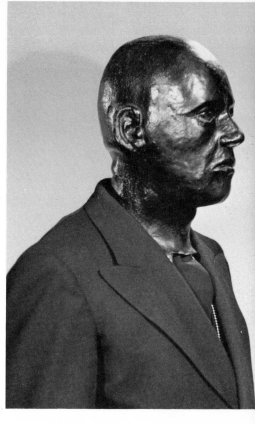

above, left: The Gargoyle was often more laughable than menacing in *The Spider Returns*
(Columbia 1941). *above, right:* The Ghost in
Dick Tracy vs. Crime, Inc. (Republic 1941)
also had the power to become invisible. *left:*
The Crimson Ghost (Republic 1946) was a
menacing antagonist with his deadly "cyclotrode"

above: The Black Hangman appears to have the advantage over Charles Trowbridge in *Adventures of the Flying Cadets* (Universal 1943). *below:* The Lightning, chief opponent of the *Fighting Devil Dogs* (Republic 1938), orders his men to fire an "electrical fire bolt."

Dennis Moore, Gregg Barton, and Lee Roberts were the stars of Columbia's final serial, *Blazing the Overland Trail* (Columbia 1956).

17. The Final Episode

HAVING ALREADY WITNESSED the death throes of pulp fiction and the glorious days of radio adventure, it was another minor traumatic experience to watch the serial fade into obscurity. After more than forty years of continuous production, no longer would anxious youths run to their favorite theatres to watch bigger-than-life heroes tackle supreme apostles of evil.

There were several important reasons for the death of the serials. Chief among these, of course, was the problem of economics. In the early days serials could be turned out relatively inexpensively, most of them being primarily shot outdoors. However, as the years progressed and production costs rose, the serial format began to look less and less appealing to the cost-conscious producer. And serials, on the whole, never really created that much revenue. The average episode was rented to a theatre for only a few dollars as an incentive to take additional features from the producing company. Those few dollars did mount up eventually, but as the years progressed the number of theatres running serials dwindled from thousands to a matter of hundreds.

When serials had reached a new peak of popularity in the early forties, it was thought that there would always be a market for the weekly adventures. Unfortunately, the people who believed this had not reckoned on television. With the growth of that all-seeing eye, youngsters could now watch complete action adventures right at home. Adventure series like *Dick Tracy, Sky King, Sergeant Preston of the Yukon, The Cisco Kid, Hopalong Cassidy, The Gene Autry Show, The Roy Rogers Show, The Lone Ranger*, etc., provided the young viewers with all the action material necessary to keep them satisfied.

There was an additional problem that confronted the serial-makers. Serials had always been filled with assorted violence and mayhem. Now the mothers and professional psychologists were beginning to attack the Saturday cliff-hangers on a rather broad front, claiming they were inducing every conceivable form of nervous ailment from extreme trauma to ringworm. The same rather vague reasons proffered by the same rather vague people caused serials to be canceled when they were shown on television in later years. All this, of course, was despite the fact that the serials provided a basic moral truth: "good always triumphs over evil." There were never any delicate shadings of purpose in the serials. The villains were *all* bad and deserved the violent fates decreed them, and the heroes were *all* good and deserved the right to mete out justice. Now, of course, we are told that life is not all good or all bad but spans the complete range between the two. I think I

155

would have hated to believe, many years ago when I sat in my favorite theatre watching *The Adventures of Captain Marvel*, that the Scorpion was a victim of a deprived childhood and that he wore his mask as an act of visual hostility towards a society which found no place in its overall scheme for him and his kind. Now *that* would have really given me a trauma.

Universal Pictures, whose serial-production history went back into the earliest days of silent films, was the first studio to realize the chapter plays had had it. The studio which had turned out such superior action fare as *Flash Gordon*, *Ace Drummond*, *Buck Rogers*, and so many favorites of the late thirties now found its market too limited for the costs involved and canceled further production after 1946. It was, perhaps, just as well, for the quality of their productions had slipped to the point where there was so little action and excitement that it was more of a chore than a pleasure to watch them. Universal had always stressed in their serials plot rather than action, and some of their serials were so talky that you simply couldn't follow what was going on half the time. When *Mysterious Mr. M* brought the Universal serial line to a close, fans viewed the demise with mixed emotions. The plot of *Mysterious Mr. M* found federal agent Grant Farrell (Dennis Moore) assisting a local plainclothesman (Richard Martin) in solving the disappearance of a famous inventor specializing in undersea devices. After thirteen dull episodes the mystery man turned out to be exactly who viewers thought it was in chapter one.

Feeling was more pronounced when Republic finally threw in the towel with *King of the Carnival* in 1955. Even at the end, though economy was all too evident, there was still enough interest (this final serial did have a mystery man) and excitement to satisfy the viewer who was not spoiled by those earlier action classics. Republic, unlike Universal and Columbia, had stockpiled nearly fifteen years of wonderful special effects built especially for their serials and features by Howard Lydecker and his special-effects department. Unlike the cheap newsreel footage constantly integrated in serials at Universal, these spectacular miniatures seemed as thrilling in 1955 as they had in 1945 or earlier. Spliced into new footage, admittedly slower and more routine, the chapter endings were still appealing and continued to bring audiences back week after week. In the great days of the studio as many as seven writers were involved in writing the fast-moving screenplay for a single serial (*Captain America*), and chapters ran up to sixteen or seventeen minutes each, with first episodes running as long as thirty minutes. The final thirteen serials turned out by the studio were written entirely by one writer, Ronald Davidson, and the running time per episode had been reduced to a standard thirteen minutes with a twenty-minute first chapter. The great days of free-swinging fights in which complete sets were demolished were a thing of the past. Fights were now done in small, cramped sets with the stunt men moving at a pace considerably slower than in years gone by. *King of the Carnival* found high-wire acrobats Harry Lauter and Fran Bennett on the trail of a counterfeiting ring operating in the circus in which they were employed. The mystery man was either seen roaming around in a clown costume or heard giving instructions to his henchmen via a two-way radio. Again, there was only one likely suspect for the mystery man. In an exciting finale, the villain is unmasked and plunges to his death after a thrilling chase, thus ending his reign of terror and bringing to a close the serial output of Republic Pictures Corporation.

Columbia decided to ring down their final curtain with the customary cheapness expected from them; they chose a Western, *Blazing the Overland Trail*, and a very routine one at that. The pedestrian plot found evil Rance Devlin (Don C. Harvey) planning to create a private army to take over the territory. Opposing him were Lee Roberts and Dennis Moore (Moore had the dubious distinction of appearing in the final serials of both Universal and Columbia). The film was so full of stock from earlier serials and features that it was hard to accept it as a new attraction. Spencer Gordon Bennet, who had directed more sound serials than any other director, including the thrill-packed *Secret Service in Darkest Africa*, *The Masked Marvel*, *Haunted Harbor*, and others, for Republic, and over twenty assorted titles for Columbia, seemed a fitting choice to bring the life of the serial, now in its terminal stage, to a peaceful and routine end. Released in 1956, *Blazing the Overland Trail* climaxed an uninterrupted flow of silent and sound serials which totaled more than five hundred titles spanning a period of forty-odd years.

Except for occasional screening on television, or a very rare re-issue to theatres, the younger generation is unable to see and enjoy these wonderful products of a vanished era. It is really a pity, for every child should be allowed to enjoy his own precious Days of Thrills and Adventure while those fleeting days of youthful escapism are still available to him.

right: Pamela Blake and Dennis Moore tried to uncover the *Mysterious Mr. M* (Universal 1946), in Universal's last serial effort. *below:* That's Harry Lauter lying on the tracks in one of the oldest serial endings. Although *King of the Carnival* (Republic 1955) had a mystery man and utilized some good stock endings, it was a poor finale to the serial output of the greatest of the serial-making studios.

A display ad for the revival of *The Adventures of Captain Marvel* (Republic 1941) in 1966 at the Trans-Lux 49th St. Theatre in New York. Notice the misspelling, of "Scorpion" and "villains"!

18. The Great Serial Revival of 1965-66

TRYING TO FORECAST motion picture trends is almost impossible. The public is, and always has been, fickle and unpredictable. Thus it was a complete surprise to all serial fans when the Batman craze burst on the horizon in late 1965. The "camp" mania was in full bloom, old movie-star posters glared out at us from hundreds of store windows, and film festivals were sprouting up all over the place. Some ambitious young entrepreneur in Chicago decided to book all fifteen chapters of the 1943 Columbia serial, *The Batman*, for a single after-midnight screening. The serial, ludicrous in its stereotyped casting of the Japanese villain, portrayed by J. Carrol Naish, and ill-costumed heroes, Lewis Wilson as Batman and Douglas Croft as Robin, the Boy Wonder, was so funny, and received so much notoriety because of the screening, that Columbia decided to reissue the entire fifteen-chapter serial to theatres in a major re-release. New ads proudly proclaimed: "Made in 1943 . . . . Discovered in 1965! Columbia Pictures presents An Evening with Batman and Robin. The greatest serial ever filmed . . . now the In-ter-tainment scoop of the year." Even *Time* magazine focused on the phenomenon, and the November 26, 1965 issue proclaimed, "Two high-camp folk heroes in a marathon of fist-fights, zombies & Ravenous Alligators!" The nation's response to the reissue was, indeed, phenom-

enal. The grosses were tremendous, and a sequel to the first serial, *Batman and Robin*, had its fifteen episodes split into two sections which were shown in dozens of theatres on succeeding Saturday matinees.

Republic Pictures Corporation, with a vault full of the best action serials, made up new prints of the 1941 *The Adventures of Captain Marvel* and the 1942 *Spy Smasher*. These two serials, both based on comic-strip heroes, were felt to be the most likely to follow the successful pattern of the Columbia reissues. Unfortunately, the release of *The Adventures of Captain Marvel* failed to achieve any notable success at all. Republic was crestfallen. Why had a superior product failed? Well, the answer was just *that* simple. When audiences had packed into the theatres to see Batman in action, they were prepared to laugh at a film that was basically ludicrous in its representation on the screen. When they came to see Captain Marvel, they had expected to do the same, but didn't. *The Adventures of Captain Marvel* was just too well made to laugh at. They did find themselves laughing *with* it, however, and enjoying it as superior screen escapism from another era. Republic chalked up the experiment as a failure, and *Spy Smasher* never saw the light of a carbon arc.

There was also another reason for the success of *The Batman* reissue. Right to this very day, the Batman is still a regularly distributed comic-book character, appearing every month on the newsstands. Captain Marvel was withdrawn from circulation over fifteen years ago when Fawcett Publications, distributor of the character's adventures, lost a multi-million-dollar suit to National Periodicals, who claimed that the Captain Marvel character was a direct steal from their Superman. Thus, a whole generation of younger filmgoers had never heard of Captain Marvel, while they were completely familiar with Batman.

Republic did derive some subsidiary benefits from the serial craze, however. They re-edited twenty-six of their serials into 100-minute feature versions and made them available to television in a package labeled "Century 66." Many stations continue to play the package even today, although many of the versions vary in quality from excellent to ridiculous. The major problem in editing a fifteen-episode serial is to maintain the continuity and retain most of the action sequences. (One of the sillier complications occurs when characters who have been killed off reappear any number of times thereafter. When episodes were spaced weeks apart, memories were slow to recall who had been killed, and who had appeared in earlier episodes. Stunt man Fred Graham gets killed and reappears at least five or six times in *D-Day on Mars*, the feature version of *The Purple Monster Strikes*.)

Based on the success of the "camp" reissue, Twentieth Century-Fox acquired television rights to the Batman character and went into full-scale production after the series was sold to the American Broadcasting Company. Unfortunately, the character was portrayed on a childish, comic-strip level and held little interest for the serial lover who had hoped for a throwback to the great action days of the forties. The only real interest lay in the casting of name actors and actresses as the villains. Burgess Meredith was a superb Penguin and Cesar Romero was equally delightful in portraying the Joker.

The following season, the Green Hornet was brought to the television screen in a somewhat straighter fashion, played for action rather than laughs. It just didn't catch on and was dropped after only one season.

Merchandising on Batman and Green Hornet items was enormously successful, almost to the point of oversaturation. In a way we were glad to see them both go, and go they did at a rather rapid pace. That fickle public again!

One other side effect based on the success of the original reissue was the release of an abridged version of *The Batman* serial in eight-millimeter film for the home market. Sales were tremendous and encouraged Republic to place a number of its condensed serial versions out in the small-size film also.

And how about the birth of *new* serials? Will some creative young genius suddenly "discover" that you can make films that are exciting and which move, rather than films which are static and overly talky? How about a serial made in the ultimate creative process—3-D? Can you visualize a theatre audience watching a blazing car plunge into its midst, or a bursting dam flooding the middle aisles? The very thought causes the pulse to quicken and the mind to boggle.

There is a definite market for the serial, even if it is only in eight millimeter. One enterprising film-maker has actually produced and marketed a new four-chapter serial satirizing the old Republic style. Louis McMahon's *Captain Celluloid vs. The Film Pirates* may be the prototype of a whole new field of home-movie entertainment. The quality of film and cameras has become so excellent in recent years that cinema buffs may soon start a new type of film production aimed directly at the home movie market.

above, left: Young Douglas Croft was Robin, the Boy Wonder in *The Batman* (Columbia 1943). *above, right:* Lewis Wilson as *The Batman* (Columbia 1943). *below:* J. Carrol Naish was an incredibly stereotyped agent of the Rising Sun in *The Batman* (Columbia 1943).

Appendix

COMPLETE LIST OF SOUND SERIALS

(arranged chronologically by studio)

REPUBLIC PICTURES CORPORATION

TITLE	STAR	NO. OF EPISODES	YEAR
1. *Darkest Africa*	Clyde Beatty	15	1936
2. *Undersea Kingdom*	Ray "Crash" Corrigan	12	
3. *The Vigilantes Are Coming*	Robert Livingston	12	
4. *Robinson Crusoe of Clipper Island*	Mala	14	
5. *Dick Tracy*	Ralph Byrd	15	1937
6. *The Painted Stallion*	Ray Corrigan	12	
7. *S.O.S. Coast Guard*	Ralph Byrd	12	
8. *Zorro Rides Again*	John Carroll	12	
9. *The Lone Ranger*	Lee Powell	15	1938
10. *Fighting Devil Dogs*	Lee Powell	12	
11. *Dick Tracy Returns*	Ralph Byrd	15	
12. *Hawk of the Wilderness*	Herman Brix	12	
13. *The Lone Ranger Rides Again*	Robert Livingston	15	1939
14. *Daredevils of the Red Circle*	Charles Quigley	12	
15. *Dick Tracy's G-Men*	Ralph Byrd	15	
16. *Zorro's Fighting Legion*	Reed Hadley	12	
17. *Drums of Fu Manchu*	Henry Brandon	15	1940
18. *Adventures of Red Ryder*	Don "Red" Barry	12	
19. *King of the Royal Mounted*	Allan Lane	12	
20. *Mysterious Dr. Satan*	Eduardo Ciannelli	15	
21. *The Adventures of Captain Marvel*	Tom Tyler	12	1941
22. *Jungle Girl*	Frances Gifford	15	
23. *King of the Texas Rangers*	"Slingin' Sammy" Baugh	12	
24. *Dick Tracy vs. Crime, Inc.*	Ralph Byrd	15	
25. *Spy Smasher*	Kane Richmond	12	1942

TITLE	STAR	NO. OF EPISODES	YEAR
26. *Perils of Nyoka*	Kay Aldridge	15	
27. *King of the Mounties*	Allan Lane	12	
28. *G-Men vs. The Black Dragon*	Rod Cameron	15	1943
29. *Daredevils of the West*	Allan Lane	12	
30. *Secret Service in Darkest Africa*	Rod Cameron	15	
31. *The Masked Marvel*	William Forrest	12	
32. *Captain America*	Dick Purcell	15	1944
33. *The Tiger Woman*	Allan Lane	12	
34. *Haunted Harbor*	Kane Richmond	15	
35. *Zorro's Black Whip*	George J. Lewis	12	
36. *Manhunt of Mystery Island*	Richard Bailey	15	1945
37. *Federal Operator 99*	Marten Lamont	12	
38. *The Purple Monster Strikes*	Dennis Moore	15	
39. *The Phantom Rider*	Robert Kent	12	1946
40. *King of the Forest Rangers*	Larry Thompson	12	
41. *Daughter of Don Q*	Adrian Booth	12	
42. *The Crimson Ghost*	Charles Quigley	12	
43. *Son of Zorro*	George Turner	13	1947
44. *Jesse James Rides Again*	Clayton Moore	13	
45. *The Black Widow*	Bruce Edwards	13	
46. *G-Men Never Forget*	Clayton Moore	12	1948
47. *Dangers of the Canadian Mounted*	Jim Bannon	12	
48. *Adventures of Frank and Jesse James*	Clayton Moore	13	
49. *Federal Agents vs. Underworld, Inc.*	Kirk Alyn	12	1949
50. *Ghost of Zorro*	Clayton Moore	12	
51. *King of the Rocket Men*	Tristram Coffin	12	
52. *The James Brothers of Missouri*	Keith Richards	12	1950
53. *Radar Patrol vs. Spy King*	Kirk Alyn	12	
54. *The Invisible Monster*	Richard Webb	12	
55. *Desperadoes of the West*	Richard Powers	12	
56. *Flying Disc Man from Mars*	Walter Reed	12	1951
57. *Don Daredevil Rides Again*	Ken Curtis	12	
58. *Government Agents vs. Phantom Legion*	Walter Reed	12	
59. *Radar Men from the Moon*	George Wallace	12	1952
60. *Zombies of the Stratosphere*	Judd Holdren	12	
61. *Jungle Drums of Africa*	Clay Moore	12	1953
62. *Canadian Mounties vs. Atomic Invaders*	Bill Henry	12	
63. *Trader Tom of the China Seas*	Harry Lauter	12	1954
64. *Man with the Steel Whip*	Richard Simmons	12	
65. *Panther Girl of the Kongo*	Phyllis Coates	12	1955
66. *King of the Carnival*	Harry Lauter	12	

COLUMBIA PICTURES CORPORATION

TITLE	STAR	NO. OF EPISODES	YEAR
1. *Jungle Menace*	Frank Buck	15	1937
2. *The Mysterious Pilot*	Captain Frank Hawks	15	
3. *The Secret of Treasure Island*	Don Terry	15	1938
4. *The Great Adventures of Wild Bill Hickok*	Gordon Elliott	15	
5. *The Spider's Web*	Warren Hull	15	
6. *Flying G-Men*	Robert Paige	15	1939
7. *Mandrake the Magician*	Warren Hull	12	
8. *Overland with Kit Carson*	Bill Elliott	15	
9. *The Shadow*	Victor Jory	15	1940
10. *Terry and the Pirates*	William Tracy	15	
11. *Deadwood Dick*	Don Douglas	15	

TITLE	STAR	NO. OF EPISODES	YEAR
12. *The Green Archer*	Victor Jory	15	
13. *White Eagle*	Buck Jones	15	1941
14. *The Spider Returns*	Warren Hull	15	
15. *The Iron Claw*	Charles Quigley	15	
16. *Holt of the Secret Service*	Jack Holt	15	
17. *Captain Midnight*	Dave O'Brien	15	1942
18. *Perils of the Royal Mounted*	Robert Stevens	15	
19. *The Secret Code*	Paul Kelly	15	
20. *The Valley of Vanishing Men*	Bill Elliott	15	
21. *The Batman*	Lewis Wilson	15	1943
22. *The Phantom*	Tom Tyler	15	
23. *The Desert Hawk*	Gilbert Roland	15	1944
24. *Black Arrow*	Robert Scott	15	
25. *Brenda Starr, Reporter*	Joan Woodbury	13	1945
26. *The Monster and the Ape*	Robert Lowery	15	
27. *Jungle Raiders*	Kane Richmond	15	
28. *Who's Guilty?*	Robert Kent	15	
29. *Hop Harrigan*	William Bakewell	15	1946
30. *Chick Carter, Detective*	Lyle Talbot	15	
31. *Son of the Guardsman*	Robert Shaw	15	
32. *Jack Armstrong*	John Hart	15	1947
33. *The Vigilante*	Ralph Byrd	15	
34. *The Sea Hound*	Buster Crabbe	15	
35. *Brick Bradford*	Kane Richmond	15	
36. *Tex Granger*	Robert Kellard	15	1948
37. *Superman*	Kirk Alyn	15	
38. *Congo Bill*	Don McGuire	15	
39. *Bruce Gentry*	Tom Neal	15	1949
40. *Batman and Robin*	Robert Lowery	15	
41. *Adventures of Sir Galahad*	George Reeves	15	
42. *Cody of the Pony Express*	Jock O'Mahoney	15	1950
43. *Atom Man vs. Superman*	Kirk Alyn	15	
44. *Pirates of the High Seas*	Buster Crabbe	15	
45. *Roar of the Iron Horse*	Jock O'Mahoney	15	1951
46. *Mysterious Island*	Richard Crane	15	
47. *Captain Video*	Judd Holdren	15	
48. *King of the Congo*	Buster Crabbe	15	1952
49. *Blackhawk*	Kirk Alyn	15	
50. *Son of Geronimo*	Clay Moore	15	
51. *The Lost Planet*	Judd Holdren	15	1953
52. *The Great Adventures of Captain Kidd*	Richard Crane	15	
53. *Gunfighters of the Northwest*	Jack Mahoney	15	1954
54. *Riding with Buffalo Bill*	Marshall Reed	15	
55. *Adventures of Captain Africa*	John Hart	15	1955
56. *Perils of the Wilderness*	Dennis Moore	15	1956
57. *Blazing the Overland Trail*	Lee Roberts	15	

UNIVERSAL PICTURES

1. *Ace of Scotland Yard* *silent & part-talkie versions*	Crauford Kent	10	1929
2. *Tarzan, the Tiger silent & sound versions*	Frank Merrill	15	
3. *The Jade Box silent & sound versions*	Jack Perrin	10	1930
4. *Lightning Express silent & sound versions*	Louise Lorraine	10	
5. *Terry of the Times silent & sound versions*	Reed Howes	10	

TITLE	STAR	NO. OF EPISODES	YEAR
6. *The Indians Are Coming* *all-talkie and silent versions*	Tim McCoy	12	
7. *Finger Prints*	Kenneth Harlan	10	*1931*
8. *Heroes of the Flames*	Tim McCoy	12	
9. *Danger Island*	Kenneth Harlan	12	
10. *Battling with Buffalo Bill*	Tom Tyler	12	
11. *Spell of the Circus*	Francis X. Bushman, Jr.	10	
12. *Detective Lloyd*	Jack Lloyd	12	*1932*
13. *The Airmail Mystery*	James Flavin	12	
14. *Heroes of the West*	Noah Beery, Jr.	12	
15. *Jungle Mystery*	Tom Tyler	12	
16. *The Lost Special*	Frank Albertson	12	
17. *Clancy of the Mounted*	Tom Tyler	12	*1933*
18. *The Phantom of the Air*	Tom Tyler	12	
19. *Gordon of Ghost City*	Buck Jones	12	
20. *The Perils of Pauline*	Evalyn Knapp	12	*1934*
21. *Pirate Treasure*	Richard Talmadge	12	
22. *The Vanishing Shadow*	Onslow Stevens	12	
23. *The Red Rider*	Buck Jones	15	
24. *Tailspin Tommy*	Maurice Murphy	12	
25. *The Rustlers of Red Dog*	John Mack Brown	12	*1935*
26. *The Call of the Savage*	Noah Beery, Jr.	12	
27. *The Roaring West*	Buck Jones	15	
28. *Tailspin Tommy in the Great Air Mystery*	Clark Williams	12	
29. *The Adventures of Frank Merriwell*	Don Briggs	12	*1936*
30. *Flash Gordon*	Buster Crabbe	13	
31. *The Phantom Rider*	Buck Jones	15	
32. *Ace Drummond*	John King	13	
33. *Jungle Jim*	Grant Withers	12	*1937*
34. *Secret Agent X-9*	Scott Kolk	12	
35. *Wild West Days*	John Mack Brown	13	
36. *Radio Patrol*	Grant Withers	12	
37. *Tim Tyler's Luck*	Frankie Thomas	12	
38. *Flash Gordon's Trip to Mars*	Buster Crabbe	15	*1938*
39. *Flaming Frontiers*	John Mack Brown	15	
40. *Red Barry*	Buster Crabbe	13	
41. *Scouts to the Rescue*	Jackie Cooper	12	*1939*
42. *Buck Rogers*	Buster Crabbe	12	
43. *The Oregon Trail*	John Mack Brown	15	
44. *The Phantom Creeps*	Bela Lugosi	12	
45. *The Green Hornet*	Gordon Jones	13	*1940*
46. *Flash Gordon Conquers the Universe*	Buster Crabbe	12	
47. *Winners of the West*	Dick Foran	13	
48. *Junior G-Men*	The Dead End Kids	12	
49. *The Green Hornet Strikes Again*	Warren Hull	15	
50. *Sky Raiders*	Donald Woods	12	*1941*
51. *Riders of Death Valley*	Dick Foran	15	
52. *Sea Raiders*	The Dead End Kids	12	
53. *Don Winslow of the Navy*	Don Terry	12	*1942*
54. *Gang Busters*	Kent Taylor	13	
55. *Junior G-Men of the Air*	The Dead End Kids	12	
56. *Overland Mail*	Lon Chaney, Jr.	15	
57. *The Adventures of Smilin' Jack*	Tom Brown	13	*1943*
58. *Don Winslow of the Coast Guard*	Don Terry	13	

TITLE	STAR	NO. OF EPISODES	YEAR
59. *Adventures of the Flying Cadets*	Johnny Downs	13	
60. *The Great Alaskan Mystery*	Ralph Morgan	13	
61. *Raiders of Ghost City*	Dennis Moore	13	*1944*
62. *Mystery of the River Boat*	Robert Lowery	13	
63. *Jungle Queen*	Lois Collier	13	
64. *The Master Key*	Milburn Stone	13	*1945*
65. *Secret Agent X-9*	Lloyd Bridges	13	
66. *The Royal Mounted Rides Again*	Bill Kennedy	13	
67. *The Scarlet Horseman*	Peter Cookson	13	*1946*
68. *Lost City of the Jungle*	Russell Hayden	13	
69. *The Mysterious Mr. M*	Richard Martin	13	

MASCOT PICTURES

1. *King of the Kongo* silent & part-talkie versions	Walter Miller	10	*1929*
2. *The Lone Defender*	Rin-Tin-Tin	12	*1930*
3. *Phantom of the West*	Tom Tyler	10	
4. *King of the Wild*	Walter Miller	12	
5. *The Vanishing Legion*	Harry Carey	12	*1931*
6. *The Galloping Ghost*	Harold "Red" Grange	12	
7. *Lightning Warrior*	Rin-Tin-Tin	12	
8. *Shadow of the Eagle*	John Wayne	12	*1932*
9. *The Last of the Mohicans*	Harry Carey	12	
10. *Hurricane Express*	John Wayne	12	
11. *The Devil Horse*	Harry Carey	12	
12. *The Whispering Shadow*	Bela Lugosi	12	*1933*
13. *The Three Musketeers*	John Wayne	12	
14. *Fighting with Kit Carson*	John Mack Brown	12	
15. *Wolf Dog*	Rin-Tin-Tin, Jr.	12	
16. *Mystery Squadron*	Bob Steele	12	
17. *The Lost Jungle*	Clyde Beatty	12	*1934*
18. *Burn 'Em Up Barnes*	Jack Mulhall	12	
19. *Law of the Wild*	Rin-Tin-Tin, Jr.	12	
20. *Mystery Mountain*	Ken Maynard	12	
21. *The Phantom Empire*	Gene Autry	12	*1935*
22. *The Miracle Rider*	Tom Mix	15	
23. *Adventures of Rex and Rinty*	Rin-Tin-Tin, Jr.	12	
24. *The Fighting Marines*	Grant Withers	12	

INDEPENDENT SERIALS

1. *Voice from the Sky* (Ben Wilson release)	Wally Wales	10	*1930*
2. *Mystery Trooper* (Syndicate Pictures Corp. release)	Robert Frazer	10	*1931*
3. *Sign of the Wolf* (Metropolitan release)	Rex Lease	10	
4. *The Last Frontier* (RKO-Radio release)	Lon Chaney, Jr.	12	*1932*
5. *Tarzan, the Fearless* (Principal release)	Buster Crabbe	12	*1933*

Appendix

TITLE	STAR	NO. OF EPISODES	YEAR
6. *Return of Chandu* *(Principal release)*	Bela Lugosi	12	*1934*
7. *Young Eagles* *(First Division)*	Jim Vance	12	
8. *Queen of the Jungle* *(Screen Attractions Corp. release)*	Reed Howes	12	*1935*
9. *The Lost City* *(Krellberg release)*	Kane Richmond	12	
10. *The New Adventures of Tarzan* *(Burroughs-Tarzan release)*	Herman Brix	12	
11. *Custer's Last Stand* *(Stage and Screen release)*	Rex Lease	15	*1936*
12. *The Clutching Hand* *(Stage and Screen release)*	Jack Mulhall	15	
13. *The Black Coin* *(Stage and Screen release)*	Ralph Graves	15	
14. *Shadow of Chinatown* *(Victory release)*	Bela Lugosi	15	
15. *Blake of Scotland Yard* *(Victory release)*	Ralph Byrd	15	*1937*